The Fleet Book

ISBN 978-1-911268-33-8
Produced and designed by Marc-Antoine Bombail & Miles Cowsill
Ship illustrations: ©Marc-Antoine Bombail (www.mab-creations.ch)

Published by Ferry Publications trading as Lily Publications Ltd
PO Box 33, Ramsey, Isle of Man, British Isles, IM99 4LP
Tel: +44 (0)1624 898 446 • Fax: +44 (0)1624 898 449

Printed and bound by Gomer Press Ltd., Wales, UK • +44 (0)1559 362 371 • © 2019 Ferry Publications trading as Lily Publications Ltd
First published in December 2018
2nd edition • Published: October 2019

Ferry
Publications

Contents

The Authors:

Miles Cowsill *was brought up in South Wales and has always had a passion for ferries of the British Isles and Europe. In the process he has amassed a vast collection of photographs and other memorabilia, and is himself an accomplished photographer taking pictures of shipping from the early seventies.*

Marc-Antoine Bombail *is a Swiss-French graphic designer and illustrator with a passion for sea travel and passenger ships. He has been creating many designs for Cunard since the early 2000's and published several books about the company. He is also specialised in drawing detailed profiles of ships, such as those reproduced in this book.*

A mon père Jacques
(1931–2018)

Marc-Antoine

The Armorique *at speed.*

Introduction

When it comes to ships, Brittany Ferries have a comfortable lead.

Prince of Brittany

This latest addition to the Brittany Ferries Fleet carries 1,000 passengers and 220 cars. There are 561 sleeping berths in 2, 3 and 4-berth cabins: many with shower and toilet, and 238 comfortable reclining seats. It is extremely well-appointed, with a help-yourself restaurant, a café, and a children's playroom. Two bars, one with a disco, and duty-free facilities. Service speed 20 knots.

Armorique

Refurbished for 1979, this ship can take up to 700 passengers and 170 cars. There's now a new restaurant and self-service cafeteria. There are 420 berths, cabins are mainly two-berth. All cabins have their own wash-basin, and many have shower and toilet. Also available, 244 reclining seats. Other facilities include a café, lounge bar, cinema and colour television lounge. Children's playroom and duty-free shops. The Armorique's service speed is 20 knots.

Cornouailles

The custom-built Cornouailles can take up to 500 passengers, in 244 berths and 100 reclining seats, as well as 200 cars. It has a spacious help-yourself restaurant, seating 230, lounge-bar, duty-free shops, colour television and a service speed of 19 knots.

Penn ar Bed

The extensively refitted Penn ar Bed now carries 420 passengers, with 230 berths in 2- or 4-berth cabins. 154 reclining seats and space for 160 cars, as well as a help-yourself restaurant, colour television lounge, lounge bar and duty-free shops. Its service speed is 18.5 knots.

Since its inception, Brittany Ferries' ambitions have remained within its core heartland, retaining strong links with the French communities from which it was spawned. Continuity of management and a local focus have been key elements in helping deliver their leading market position, coupled with an investment programme that has continued to deliver a fleet tailored to meet changing customer needs. The quality of the fleet has been matched by consistency of award-winning on board service, creating strong customer loyalty and advocacy, allowing the company to withstand the buffeting of competition and the vagaries of the market.

This volume provides a wealth of background information about the vessels, but success has been based on much more than having the right ships – placing them on the right routes at the right time has been crucial to building and maintaining Brittany Ferries' market dominance.

From the very beginning, the operational philosophy of Brittany Ferries was clearly differentiated from its competitors. Early cross-channel services were established by British and French railway companies, taking passengers and freight to destinations that provided onward rail connections, particularly to Paris. Time at sea was minimised, as the sea journey was more to be endured than enjoyed, but this gave the operational advantage of optimising vessel utilisation. As the holiday and freight markets matured towards greater use of motor vehicles, so this traditional route approach became increasingly out-dated.

In 1973 the nearest cross-channel competition to the fledgling Brittany Ferries operation was provided by Thoresen Car Ferries and Sealink (from 1974) operating between the traditional railway ports of Southampton, Weymouth, Le Havre and Cherbourg, sufficiently remote from Plymouth to be seen as

serving a separate market. As Brittany Ferries expanded they established a route network based on ports that no longer – or never - had ferry services, using the logic of freight flows, holiday destinations and geography to determine the appropriateness of destinations. The pioneering of Portsmouth and Poole as operational bases, the re-opening of St Malo, the growth of services to Santander and - especially - the development of Ouistreham (Caen), all characterised the Brittany Ferries approach. Whilst Townsend Thoresen considered a route to Ouistreham, this bisected their established services to the freight port of Le Havre and the tourist destination of Cherbourg. So the way was clear for Brittany Ferries to build their new service direct to the heart of Normandy, taking traffic from both competing routes.

This market-driven perspective enabled the new company to break free from the restrictions of their competitors' union dominated seafaring and port handling staff. Brittany Ferries had a clear regional identity, associating itself closely with a holiday product that attracted a loyal clientele. Here again, Brittany Ferries distinguished itself from other companies. Whilst competing operators – including P&O European Ferries, Sealink and Hoverspeed – had the advantage of belonging to larger groups with operational interests spread across a wider network, Western Channel services were a small and often loss-making portion of their portfolio. The profitability of short-sea routes drove their businesses and the interests of other routes were subsumed to the wider corporate good. With no interests outside the Western Channel, Brittany Ferries was able to maintain a clear specialist focus on the needs of that

Right: The Penn Ar Bed.

market sector. The world of the £1 'booze cruise' was not one that Brittany Ferries wished to inhabit.

Brittany Ferries also never forgot that the ferry crossing was only a means to an end. Having developed a strong mix of routes and a fleet of modern purpose-designed vessels, the company understood that its clients were only travelling to reach holiday destinations. Providing a ferry-inclusive holiday product from 1978 to create one of the largest such businesses in France, and developing a Property Owners' Club, were key steps in further differentiating the company from competition, and helped create and retain customer loyalty. Customers could book their holiday, travel aboard the fleet, enjoy quality on-board catering and arrive as close as possible to their destination after a restful, comfortable crossing with all aspects of the experience delivered and controlled by Brittany Ferries. The holiday product expanded to cover gites, and these proved especially popular. Other operators found it difficult to compete directly, as they were nervous of upsetting the inclusive-holiday companies who were vital to their interests on other routes.

Local focus was evident in the design of the first two bespoke vessels for the company – *Penn Ar Bed*

and *Cornouailles*. Of necessity at the time they were built to accommodate the agricultural exports on which the operation had been founded. Passenger facilities were a secondary consideration, with limited cabin capacity and much use made of formica finishes. But great emphasis was placed on cleanliness and punctuality, and new standards were set for cross-channel sailings in the provision of freshly cooked French cuisine. Vessels were outfitted in a bright clean white livery, contrasting with the more traditional dark blue hulls sported by the Sealink fleet and the brash orange of Thoresen Car Ferries, and supporting the positioning of the company as a holiday operation. It is no coincidence that a white livery is by far the preferred colour employed by cruise vessels today.

Designs by Knud E. Hansen dominated the next six vessels brought into the fleet. The *Armorique, Prince of Brittany, Goëlo, Trégastel, Quiberon* and *Duc de Normandie* shared the same Scandinavian parentage, as Brittany Ferries expanded its operations to open up routes from Portsmouth to St Malo and Caen, and from Plymouth to Santander, between 1978 and 1985. The company made good use of its links with regional authorities in France to finance the acquisitions. The *Duc de Normandie* was the first vessel to receive a complete interior refit by Architectes Ingénieurs Associés (AIA), raising the bar in establishing on board facilities and style, and providing a basis for the future direction for the company. This culminated in designs for the *Bretagne* for the Santander route, the only new cruise-ferry built for the company in a French yard. She transformed standards on the Western Channel, and further orders for the *Normandie* and *Barfleur* for the Caen and Cherbourg routes soon followed.

The facilities and on-board environment on each vessel were tailored to the market in a way that competitors could not emulate. Momentum was now

behind Brittany Ferries, and principal competitor P&O European Ferries played 'catch-up' with charters of the *Pride of Bilbao, Pride of Le Havre* and *Pride of Portsmouth*. Chartering highlighted the structural differences in approach between Brittany Ferries and its competitors, and burdened P&O with high costs.

Brittany Ferries consolidated its leadership in the Western Channel with further investment in the *Val de Loire, Mont St Michel* and *Pont-Aven* between 1993 and 2004. Each featured a strong emphasis on regional cuisine presented through a choice of restaurants, artwork from critically-acclaimed French and Scottish artists and cultural displays reflecting the destinations served by the vessels. Over 85 per cent of passengers travelling on the Western Channel routes are British, heading for a holiday

Above: Part of the passenger lounge on the Trégastel.

Interiors of the Pont-Aven *(above) and* Armorique *(below).*

in France or Spain, and they responded positively to the Brittany Ferries shipboard environment. By clever use of local theming, Brittany Ferries was able to extend the French and Spanish holiday experience to the time spent on board the fleet, in a way that other companies could not match. The arrival of *Cap Finistère* in 2010 placed Brittany Ferries in an unassailable position. With the demise of P&O European Ferries, Sealink, Hoverspeed and LD Lines services in the Western Channel and to Spain, any future competitor faces a formidable fleet deployment, requiring risking substantial capital to have any impact. Brittany Ferries continued to future-proof its position by opening the Cork-Santander route with the *Connemara* in 2018, offering a direct service between Ireland and Spain for the first time. The forthcoming arrival of *Honfleur, Galicia, Salamanca* and *Santoña* will only enhance this formidable position.

Like many long-standing ferry operations, Brittany Ferries initially inherited a tradition of employing redundant French Merchant Navy seamen to provide on board services. Early shipboard hospitality was delivered by seafarers with few skills in their new profession and catering standards were basic, with limited menus available on board. As services expanded – particularly on the Plymouth-Santander route – so the need to emulate the traditions of French cruise-style service on long crossings became paramount. With the introduction of professional chefs from the 1980s the on board service was gradually overhauled, culminating in the definition of new service-delivery standards with the introduction of *Bretagne* in 1989, offering a wide variety of regional cuisine to suit a range of tastes and budgets. The expanded menu and aroma of freshly baked pastries, coupled with buffets of sumptuous patisseries created by on board teams of skilled pâtissiers, contributed strongly to the company regularly winning awards for quality of service such as 'Best Cross-Channel Ferry Operator' in the Daily Telegraph Travel Awards. Brittany Ferries continues to tightly define and control the menu and service delivery.

Brittany Ferries' long-term strategy to become the leading player on the Western and Central Channel, and make a significant regional contribution, has become reality. With a fleet of eleven modern ships carrying over 2.5 million passengers each year, the company is a major player in the European Ferry industry offering a network of 'Motorways of the Sea' serving the Atlantic Arc. The company still maintains traditional close partnerships with Regional Councils, tourism bodies, legal and financial experts, architects and advertising agencies, to create the special Gallic flavour that characterises their services. Brittany Ferries positions itself as an ambassador for French gastronomy and quality cuisine delivered by a team of 200 chefs. The company is now a leading French regional economic and social contributor, with 81 per cent of its purchases, storing and maintenance operations benefiting Brittany, Normandy, the Pays de Loire and Ile de France, and offers direct employment for 2,500 people, including 1,700 seafaring staff, indirectly supporting a further 4,500 jobs.

No operation of this size could be maintained if fleet standards fell short of customer expectations and appropriate levels of capacity were not available at peak periods. The enduring legacy of Brittany Ferries has been to approach expansion and investment decisions with a strong market focus, constantly honing the fleet to withstand intense competition whilst remaining integrated with the regional communities which it serves. This story is book-ended by the UK joining the European Economic Community in 1973 and choosing to leave the European Union in 2019. Brittany Ferries approach throughout this period has differed markedly from that of its competitors and a strong regional focus and identity has served the company and its customers well over the last forty-five years. The fleet investment programme continues with three new vessels to come, and there is every reason to believe that this enduring and consistent business strategy will continue to be successful.

Richard Kirkman
October 2018

A Breton Company is Born

In the early months of 1972 a group of vegetable farmers surprised the shipping world with the news that they planned to operate a ferry service between the port of Roscoff (in western Brittany) and Plymouth in Devon. Breton farmers for many years had been considering a quicker way of transporting their goods to Britain following the closure by British Rail of the Southampton–St. Malo service in 1964. British Rail decided to close the service as they claimed they could not make it pay, and the *St. Patrick* made her last sailing from St. Malo to Southampton on 27th September. It is interesting to note that during the *St. Patrick*'s last season on most of her sailings there were fewer than 100 passengers, and cargo loadings were also poor, with less than 800 tons being carried during the last year in service. Some twelve years later Brittany Ferries was to reopen the route, establishing St. Malo as an important link with Britain.

With the closure of the St. Malo service the farmers of Brittany were forced to use the other services to England from Le Havre and Cherbourg operated by Thoresen Car Ferries, who had reopened both routes following British Railways' decision to close these routes also in 1964. The ferry services from Cherbourg and Le Havre were not ideal for the transportation of vegetables to Britain due to the distance involved in transporting fresh goods, especially from western Brittany. Not only did the farmers want to get their produce to Britain faster, but they also wanted a far more economical way. Some nine years after closure of the St. Malo service, Brittany Ferries, as we know it today, was established.

Initially, the company was known as Armement Bretagne-Angleterre-Irlande (BAI). The new operation was the brainchild of Alexis Gourvennec and his fellow associates of the SICA group (an organisation set up to protect the interests of vegetable produc-ers). The newly formed company chose for its cross-Channel link the fishing harbour of Roscoff in western Brittany and the Devon port of Plymouth.

Alexis Gourvennec's initial plans envisaged a freight-only service, and the ro-ro ship *Lilac* (2,293 gross tons) was purchased for the new operation. She could accommodate 45 commercial lorries. Madame Annie Gourvennec renamed her *Kerisnel*, after a little village in Brittany famous for its cauli-flowers, on 17th December 1972.

On 2nd January 1973, with French, British and Breton flags flying and a choir singing carols, Brittany Ferries was officially born. Nearly 3,000 people attended the official opening of the terminal at Roscoff on a bleak New Year's Day. During the first three months, Brittany Ferries was to carry only 17,000 tons of traffic and not the 40,000 tons originally planned. However, like any new service it was to take time for trade to gather momentum.

Following the introduction of the new freight-only service between Roscoff and Plymouth, it quickly

The inauguration of the Kerisnel *on 2nd January 1973.*

Alexis Gourvennec at a trade exhibition during the early days of the company.

became evident that there was a demand for a passenger service to and from Brittany, which was now developing as a popular destination for British tourists. As a result of this demand, an agreement was reached between Brittany Ferries and Vedettes Armoricaines of Brest to operate a passenger-only service using a former Stena Line day-only Baltic vessel, the *Poseidon* (1,358 gross tons). The planned passenger-only service started on 19th May 1973. The passenger service sailed initially from Trinity Pier, Plymouth on Mondays, Tuesdays and Fridays to the Roscoff ferry terminal. At first the service

Right: The launch of the Penn Ar Bed.

Below: The Penn Ar Bed *at Roscoff with the* Prince de Bretagne.

was rather erratic but eventually the service settled down, and during July the *Poseidon* was to average some 120 passengers a day before she finished her summer season on 15th September 1973.

While the trial passenger service was operating, the company announced they had placed an order with a yard at La Rochelle in France to build a new ferry for the link. The ferry would be designed to carry passengers and their cars, together with freight, and it was envisaged that she would operate with the *Kerisnel* which would be converted to provide passenger accommodation for the next season.

The new ship, named *Penn Ar Bed* (Breton for Land's End), was delayed at the builders by a strike and it was not until mid January 1974 that she was able to undergo her sea trials. The new ferry had capacity for 50 freight vehicles, or a mixture of freight and cars, and accommodation for 250 passengers. With a service speed of 19 knots, she was ideal for the six-hour journey between the two ports. On 24th January the *Penn Ar Bed* (2,891 gross tons), made her maiden voyage to Plymouth.

In the light of good bookings for the following season, the first glossy brochure of the company was produced. Brittany Ferries in the following years was to provide some of the best looking holiday brochures ever produced by any ferry company. The reproduction of its colour brochures was also to heighten the British public's awareness of the beauty of Brittany and the western Loire as a holiday destination.

Brittany Ferries announced in April 1975 that it had chartered the vessel *Falster* (2,424 gross tons) for six months, with an option to purchase her if she proved to be a success. She was renamed *Prince de Bretagne*. Her charter now meant that the company was able to provide a twice-daily service between Roscoff and Plymouth.

Meanwhile, earlier in the year a number of companies had expressed interest in

Top: Bar on the Penn Ar Bed. *Below: The gift and duty-free shop on the* Penn Ar Bed.

Expansion

The trial operation proved to be a great success and it was decided to open a St. Malo route to the UK from 1976, using the newly established ferry port at Portsmouth. The ship chosen to operate the new link was the French-built *Terje Vigen* (5,732 gross tons), originally built for a service between Norway and Denmark. This Norwegian-registered ship was purchased by Brittany Ferries and underwent a major refit prior to her arrival at Plymouth on 4th March 1976. The newly acquired vessel was renamed *Armorique* and was to become the most faithful and widely travelled ship of the company in her next two decades of service. The *Armorique* was placed initially on the freight runs between Roscoff and Plymouth, and on 25th March she made her first passenger sailing. Some two weeks later she commenced passenger operations between St. Malo and Plymouth, prior to the completion of the new terminal at Portsmouth.

The *Armorique* opened the St. Malo–Portsmouth service on 17th June, using the newly completed ferry terminal. During the first season the *Armorique* sailed from St. Malo in the morning and from Portsmouth in the evening inward to Brittany.

With two ferry links from Brittany to England and three ships, the company now looked set to break new records. Such was the confidence of the company that it ordered a new ship from a Norwegian yard for delivery the following season.

Sadly, operations did not go as planned for the 1976 season. On the morning of 5th July the *Armorique* ran aground as she approached St. Malo in thick fog. One of her variable-pitch propellers was severely damaged, and with slight damage to her hull she had to be withdrawn from service for repairs at Le Havre. The *Bonanza* (2,399 gross tons), which had been chartered from Fred. Olsen for the Roscoff

The crew of the Penn Ar Bed *poses on the ship's after deck.*

re-establishing a UK–St. Malo route, including Sealink who had closed the route in 1964. Of three companies, TT-Line pursued the project and planned to open their new seasonal service from Southampton, from 28th May until 12th October, using the passenger ferry *Mary Poppins* (ex-*Gosta Berling*) which would operate five sailings a week in each direction. There was strong trade union opposition to the new service from both dockers and seamen in Britain and farmers in Brittany, as it was thought the new service to Brittany would affect the other operators in the Western Channel in the long term. The *Mary Poppins* arrived at Southampton at the end of May to open the new link. Immediately, both Townsend Thoresen and Sealink were affected by strikes in opposition to the new service, which in the event did not materialise.

In the light of this, Brittany Ferries began to investigate starting another route from Brittany to England. As an experiment during the late summer, the company operated three sailings a week from St. Malo to Plymouth from mid August to early October.

service during the summer, was switched to the St. Malo route as a temporary measure. The Norwegian ship was able to accommodate 500 passengers and 200 cars, but because she was only a day vessel, with only a few cabins, she was not ideal for the nine-hour link. Brittany Ferries made frantic efforts to find another ship in the absence of the *Armorique*, but without success, and so it was decided to switch the *Penn Ar Bed* from Roscoff as she had better accommodation. In August, the Danish ship *Olau West* (3,100 gross tons) was eventually chartered to replace the *Armorique*, while she was still under repair. Some two days later disaster also struck the chartered ship when, following her morning departure from St. Malo, she ran aground with 600 passengers on board. She grounded close to the Môle des Noires, in the outer entrance to the harbour. She was later re-floated, and when it was found that it was safe for her to continue she made her way to the UK. However, after arriving at Portsmouth, it was decided to withdraw her from service for repairs at Flushing in the Netherlands. Passengers and cars had to be transferred to sailings of Townsend Thoresen from Southampton and Portsmouth until the *Olau West* was able to resume service.

The Armorique.

The *Olau West* was far from an ideal ship for the route and Brittany Ferries was not happy with the service. As a result the link was closed on 10th October to enable the St. Malo port authorities to carry out a further programme of improvements to the approaches to the ferry port. These improvements would enable the company in future to operate all the year round and at most states of the tide.

Repairs to the *Armorique*, which were only expected to take four weeks, in fact took just over three months. Even with the problems of the season at St. Malo the route attracted some 75,000 passengers and 18,000 cars in the four months of operation. Brittany Ferries was able to see the potential of Portsmouth, with its superb road communications with other parts of Britain, and soon the company started to consider other links from the port to France.

The newly built *Cornouailles* (3,383 gross tons) entered service on 24th May 1977. Following the *Cornouailles* entering service, sailings were

increased between Roscoff and Plymouth with up to three a day being offered at weekends. In addition to the increased service on the Roscoff route, the *Penn Ar Bed* operated from 27th May between Plymouth and St. Malo at 10.00 on Monday and Tuesday with an arrival in France at 19.00. Sailings from St. Malo to Devon were offered on Monday and Friday at 23.00. During the other part of the week she supported the *Armorique* on the Portsmouth link.

In the autumn, Brittany Ferries announced further expansion plans for 1978, which were to include links to Spain from England and a new ferry service from Roscoff to Cork. A British–Spanish link had been operated by no less than three companies during the previous ten years, prior to the Breton company's decision to reopen the link between the two countries.

Brittany Ferries took the bold step of reopening the link, not from Southampton as it believed that the time at sea was too long for passengers, but instead it decided to resume the operation from Plymouth. By providing a service from Plymouth and obtaining agreement with the French government to pass close to the western coast of Brittany, the company was able to offer a 23-hour link, thereby cutting out the two nights on the ship that had been the downfall of the previous operations.

The *Armorique* was chosen to operate the twice-weekly service on Mondays and Wednesdays from Plymouth. On her return from Spain on a Friday, she would then provide an extra sailing on the Roscoff route, to enable her to be in position for a round trip to Cork at the weekends.

Meanwhile, in 1978, the *Armorique* was replaced by the chartered Swedish vessel *Prince of Fundy* (5,464 gross tons) on the St. Malo service. The ship had originally been built for Lion Ferry's new service linking Canada and the USA and had been named after the Bay of Fundy, which she crossed between

Alexis Gourvennec and Christian Michielini at the naming ceremony of the Cornouailles.

Yarmouth (Nova Scotia) and Portland (Maine). The newly chartered ship was named *Prince of Brittany* and operated the St. Malo service from 1978 with the support of the *Penn Ar Bed*. The 'Prince' proved to be a very popular vessel with the travelling public on the link and was to remain on the route for the next ten years.

The *Armorique* opened the new Plymouth–Santander route on 17th April 1978. She was to prove a popular vessel on the link. The new Spanish service was to grow very rapidly over the next ten years and gradually larger tonnage had to be introduced to

meet the increased demand. The new seasonal Irish service operated very successfully and also grew like the Spanish operation. In 1979 the Spanish service was extended to an all-the-year-round basis.

Brittany Ferries looked forward to the next season with great confidence with all the signs of increased passenger and car traffic, but sadly it was to prove a season fraught with problems. The *Armorique* was sent to Falmouth Ship Repairers for her annual refit and further improvements to her passenger accommodation prior to her reopening the Spanish service on 10th February

The Prince of Brittany *in rough seas off Alderney.*

1979. Unfortunately, she became a victim of a strike at the British yard while undergoing her refit and work was not completed on her until April. Meanwhile, the *Prince of Brittany* had to be switched to the Santander service as a temporary measure until the *Armorique* could be released from the strike at Falmouth.

It was planned for 1979 that the Roscoff–Plymouth service would be covered by the *Cornouailles*, while the *Prince of Brittany* and the *Penn Ar Bed* would work the St. Malo–Plymouth link. In addition to the *Penn Ar Bed* covering the Portsmouth service, she would also cover the seasonal service from St. Malo to Plymouth. Brittany Ferries also chartered the freight ship *Normandia* (2,311 gross tons) to cover the Cork, Plymouth and Portsmouth services. The complex web of services relied on good

The **Normandia.**

maintenance of the fleet and also good management at the ports, especially with very tight turnarounds expected between sailings. All went to plan until mid June, when three of the company's ferries broke down in succession. The *Cornouailles* was first, followed by the *Penn Ar Bed* and then the *Prince of Brittany*. As a result of the failure of the ships, the company was forced to charter the rather shabby B&I ferry *Munster* (4,067 gross tons) initially for a twenty-day period to cover the absent *Cornouailles*. The charter had to be extended when the *Prince of Brittany* then broke down. The Irish vessel was a far cry from the high standards of Brittany Ferries, and passengers boarding the ship were issued with letters apologising for the poor standard of accommodation offered on board. Eventually a more suitable vessel was found to replace the *Munster*, in the Danish-registered *Regina* (8,020 gross tons) which was chartered until the 'Prince' returned from repairs. It was later disclosed that all three ships had been plagued with similar mechanical problems when they had been refitted at a Brest shipyard. It is believed that the problems were attributed to engine bearings which had been fitted by the yard during their overhauls the previous winter.

New Ships

Three new vessels entered service with Brittany Ferries for the next season. Firstly the company decided to charter the Italian freight ship *Faraday* (2,932 gross tons) to cover the freight operations on the St. Malo route for the next season. The company also purchased the Greek freight ship *Iniochos Express* (2,768 gross tons) from Iniochos Shipping S.A. to cover the Plymouth–Santander and Roscoff operations. The ten-year-old freight ship, built in Hong Kong for the Union S.S. Co., New Zealand, was renamed *Breizh-Izel*.

Meanwhile, the summer passenger schedules from St. Malo to Portsmouth were extended in the light of a good level of bookings for the route. To meet the increased demand Brittany Ferries also chartered the *Viking 6* (5,073 gross tons) to cover the St. Malo service for the summer with the *Prince of Brittany*. The Finnish vessel was renamed *Goëlo*, after a region in north-east Brittany. She was to operate for the next two seasons on the nine-hour link. The *Goëlo* was an extremely comfortable ship, boasting high-class cabin accommodation fitted when she had been used on the Alaska cruise trade. The ship proved an excellent operating partner with the *Prince of Brittany* for the next two years.

Brittany Ferries was to have a trouble-free season until mid August when all services were disrupted by industrial action from French fishermen. The trouble started on 13th August 1980 when the first of the Channel ports were affected by the blockade, and some seven days later all French ferry ports were closed by industrial action. It was not until 21st August the *Cornouailles* broke the blockade at Roscoff; by the end of the week all the dramas were over, as the French fishermen agreed to reopen the blockaded ports to holiday traffic.

During December Brittany Ferries announced plans to charter the Fred. Olsen ship *Bolero* (11,344 gross tons) and rename her *Trégor* to expand and improve the Santander route. The plan fell through at the eleventh hour, the company claiming that the charter could not be finalised for the 1981 season.

Further financial problems came to light in late 1981 when Brittany Ferries announced that losses for 1981 would be in the region of £2.4 million.

Above: Artist's impression of the Trégor.

Below: The Goëlo.

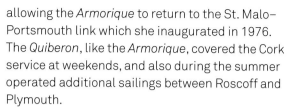

The Quiberon.

allowing the *Armorique* to return to the St. Malo–Portsmouth link which she inaugurated in 1976. The *Quiberon*, like the *Armorique*, covered the Cork service at weekends, and also during the summer operated additional sailings between Roscoff and Plymouth.

In 1983 Brittany Ferries, which had been formed to transport farm produce from Brittany to England, celebrated its tenth birthday with a fleet of six ships and four ferry services. The next ten years of the growth of the company was to be even more dramatic. The *Gelting Nord* (4,371 gross tons) was chartered as a replacement ship for the Roscoff–Plymouth service for the 1983 season in place of the *Cornouailles*. The new ship, renamed *Bénodet* after a resort in southern Brittany, entered service on 30th April. She was a major improvement over the *Cornouailles*, with more space for cars and superior cabin and passenger accommodation.

Early in the new year, the Jersey government invited another operator to compete with Sealink on the Channel Islands services from mainland Britain. By spring a consortium of Jersey-based Huelin-Renouf, Brittany Ferries and the haulage company Mainland Market Deliveries (MMD) were considering plans to start a rival service to that of Sealink between the Channel Islands and Britain, with the sale-listed *Penn Ar Bed*. The vessel was to prove unsuitable for the service, as the British Department of Trade wanted a reduction in her freight capacity under the British flag. It was decided to look elsewhere for a suitable ship, and the *Penn Ar Bed* was sold to Swedish interests for a new service across the Oslofjord. She was renamed *Sven No Marina* by her new owners, and was later sold again to Marlines in Greece and renamed *Princess M* for service in the Mediterranean.

By the end of the year, Huelin-Renouf announced that, with the backing of Brittany Ferries (27% inter-

The financial crisis had been caused by heavy borrowings for the purchase of new tonnage, and to some extent the crisis had been brought about by a price war which had raged with other ferry operators for the last two years on the English Channel. A financial package was arranged to save the company and some £8.5 million was injected into a new holding company.

Once Brittany Ferries was back on a firm financial footing and with increased demand on all the company's routes, especially on the Santander service, Brittany Ferries chartered, with an option to purchase, the *Nils Dacke* (7,950 gross tons). The German-built ship of 1975 could operate at 22.5 knots, enabling her to reduce the crossing time to Spain by some two hours during the peak season if required. The chartered ship was renamed *Quiberon*, after the peninsula and town in southern Brittany. The *Quiberon* entered service in May 1982,

est) and MMD (the principal haulage company to the Channel Islands), a new ferry service would start from March 1985, in competition with Sealink British Ferries who had held the monopoly of the Channel Islands services for most of the century. The *Bénodet* (chartered to Brittany Ferries for its Roscoff route in 1983) would open the new service from Thursday 28th March 1985. The former Brittany Ferries ship was renamed *Corbière* and was to be manned by a British crew.

Meanwhile, the *Quiberon* was purchased by Brittany Ferries at the end of 1984 following two very successful seasons on the Santander/Cork services. With the *Bénodet* now required on the new Channel Islands link, Brittany Ferries took out a three-year bareboat charter of the Yugoslav ferry *Njegos* (3,998 gross tons). The chartered vessel entered service on the Roscoff–Plymouth service on 1st May 1985 as the *Trégastel*. Prior to her arrival, the faithful *Armorique* had covered the link following the transfer of the *Bénodet*.

The Trégastel *and* Breizh-Izel *in Plymouth Sound.*

The Duc de Normandie *arriving at Roscoff.*

Further consolidation

During the summer of 1985, in the space of less than a month, Brittany Ferries announced that it had purchased the elegant Dutch ferry *Prinses Beatrix* from SMZ (the Zeeland Steamship Company), the Dutch partner in Sealink operations, for a new service between Portsmouth and Lower Normandy. This announcement was followed by the news that it had also acquired the successful freight shipping com-

pany Truckline, the freight-only operators between Poole and Cherbourg. The purchase of Truckline and their two ships was a major boost to the company.

For some time, following the decision by its rivals Townsend Thoresen at Portsmouth not to open a new ferry service to the port of Ouistreham (north of Caen), the company had been investigating a new link from Portsmouth to Normandy. Brittany Ferries was offered the new French port instead. The company could see the new terminal offered great potential and would enable it to rival the operations of Townsend Thoresen at Cherbourg and Le Havre. The new link from Normandy would operate from a new berth and terminal on the seaward side of the entrance to the canal serving Caen. The *Prinses Beatrix* (13,505 gross tons) would not only be the biggest ship of the fleet, but also the largest ferry ever to operate out of Portsmouth.

The *Prinses Beatrix* underwent a major refit in the Netherlands prior to entering service; the renamed vessel the *Duc de Normandie* entered service on 5th June 1986 on the 23.30 sailing to Normandy. Her extremely well-appointed accommodation brought a new sense of style and taste in ferry travel, which was to set new standards on the Channel, which in turn was to offer a real challenge to the other rival ferry operators. So successful was the new route, at the height of the summer season, the Truckline freight ships *Purbeck* and *Coutances* were having to assist the *Duc de Normandie* on the Caen service. The Caen operation had proved to be a great success overnight, far ahead of expectations.

Brittany Ferries invited tenders for a new purpose-built ferry for its Santander route, to meet the growing summer demand on this ferry link which was now ten years old. Brittany Ferries had hoped that it might be able to find a suitable second-hand ship, however, in the event it was unsuccessful. Following many months of speculation as to which yard would be awarded the work, Brittany Ferries finally signed contracts with the French yard of Chantiers de l'Atlantique at St. Nazaire, for delivery of the ship during the spring of 1989. The new superferry was ordered by Sabemen, a Breton shipowning investment company linked to Brittany Ferries. On her completion she would then be chartered to Brittany Ferries for 20 years. The new 24,534 gross ton vessel would be named *Bretagne* and would offer cruise-liner standards for 2,000 passengers with berths

for just over half the passengers in two and four-berth cabins and space for 600 cars. The ship would also boast 500 reclining seats in five Club Lounges, a 288-seater à la carte restaurant, a 430-seat self-service restaurant, plus a 150-seat salon de thé, two bars, a 74-seat wine bar, conference room, a duty-free supermarket and an arcade of boutiques. The *Bretagne* would be powered by four 12-cylinder Wärtsilä diesels, giving a projected service speed of 21 knots which would be sufficient on the Spanish route in most weather conditions.

Due to the overwhelming success of Channel Island Ferries, Sealink were forced into discussing a joint operation to the islands with their rivals in the light of high losses incurred by them during the two years, but the planned merger did not take place; the former nationalised ferry company withdrew from the Channel Islands services after holding the monopoly for a century. A new operating company known as British

The restaurant on the Duc de Normandie.

Channel Island Ferries (BCIF) was formed to operate the new passenger-only services between Britain and the islands. During the winter, the freight vessel *Breizh-Izel* was chartered to BCIF to provide the extra capacity now required on the link, following Sealink withdrawing their four passenger/freight vessels.

Operations for 1987 were to remain very much the same as in the previous years, with the *Quiberon* and *Trégastel* covering the western sector of operations, the *Prince of Brittany* and the *Armorique* covering the St. Malo service and the *Duc de Normandie* with the freight vessel *Purbeck* on the Caen route. With growing Irish and French passenger trade, Brittany Ferries came to an agreement with Swansea Cork Ferries to charter their vessel *Celtic Pride* once a week during the peak season, to offer extra capacity in addition to the *Quiberon*'s weekend sailing. This arrangement was repeated in 1988, prior to the arrival of the *Bretagne* the next season.

Just before the end of 1987, Brittany Ferries announced that it planned to introduce a second ship on its Caen service during the next season, from 19th May to 11th September 1988, as consort to the *Duc de Normandie*. The company took a one-year bareboat charter of the Yugoslav-built ship *Gotland*, which would offer accommodation for 1,200 passengers.

In June, Brittany Ferries announced that it had purchased the B&I ferry *Connacht* for delivery in the autumn. The newly acquired ship had been built originally for B&I in 1978 for their now defunct Cork–Pembroke Dock route. It was disclosed by Brittany Ferries that she would undergo a £2 million refit prior to her becoming the principal ship on the St. Malo route for 1989 in place of the *Prince of Brittany*, along with the *Armorique*. The company took delivery of the *Connacht* on 3rd October, after which she was sent to Papenburg in West Germany for refit before entering service.

Brittany Ferries re-organised its fleet for 1989, with the pending arrival of the *Bretagne* and the introduction of the *Duchesse Anne* on the St.Malo link. On the Caen–Portsmouth service the *Duc de Normandie* was joined by the former *Prince of Brittany*, which for her new role was renamed *Reine Mathilde* after William the Conqueror's queen. Following her extensive refit, she made her passenger debut on the route on 17th March. In addition to the extra passenger sailings offered for 1989, further freight capacity was provided by the newly chartered Truckline vessel *Normandie Shipper*.

It was also decided that the St. Malo route would be a seasonal service (mid February to mid November) instead of an all-the-year-round operation. *The Duchesse Anne*, the largest vessel to date to serve on the link, opened the new seasonal service on 13th February, and she was joined later in May by the faithful *Armorique* for an extended two-ship summer service. The *Quiberon* returned to the Plymouth–Santander route during February,

The Duchesse Anne.

following the *Armorique* reopening the 23-hour link on 15th January. It was planned that the *Quiberon* would maintain the Santander, Roscoff and Cork services until the delivery of the *Bretagne*. Following the new flagship entering service, the *Trégastel* would then transfer to the Truckline passenger route between Cherbourg and Poole and the *Quiberon* would become the main vessel of the premier route.

Enter the *Bretagne*

On 4th February 1989 the £55 million *Bretagne* was launched at St. Nazaire. The new flagship represented the spearhead part of a £70 million investment by the company to challenge the Channel Tunnel during the next decade. Following a series of frustrating delays, the new flagship *Bretagne* slipped into Plymouth Sound on 14th July, on her delivery voyage via Roscoff. Two days later she entered commercial service. Following this, the *Quiberon* was transferred as planned, which in turn allowed the *Trégastel* to move to the Truckline passenger service.

Following the introduction of the *Bretagne*, the company had a record year in 1989, with some 2.1 million passengers travelling on the six-route network. Brittany Ferries decided to expand its Truckline 'Les Routiers' service to a two-ship operation using the *Corbière* with the *Trégastel* for the next season. Up to four passenger sailings a day during the peak season would be offered, and with

The Reine Mathilde *(ex*-Prince of Brittany*) passes the* Duc de Normandie.

Top and bottom left: The Bretagne under construction.

Top right and below: The naming ceremony of the Bretagne.

the two passenger ships and two freight vessels the link was to see up to sixteen sailings a day during 1990. The company's other services were to remain very much the same for the next season.

In May 1990 Brittany Ferries announced plans to build two new vessels to replace some of the older tonnage in the fleet and to expand the Caen–Portsmouth operations. The contract for the first ferry, a new jumbo ship for the Caen service, was awarded to Kvaerner Masa Yards at Helsinki in Finland. A second ship for the Truckline passenger operation was also later secured with Masa at Turku. Both orders were worth some £130 million; each vessel was to take two years to build and would be built to the new 1990 SOLAS specifications, with designs reflecting the latest international thinking on safety at sea.

Setting new standards on the English Channel

The first of the new vessels being built in Finland, the *Barfleur* for the Truckline service, took to the water on 26th July 1991. The 18,000 gross ton superferry, when completed, would be able to take 1,200 passengers and 270 cars, or in an all-freight configuration 118 freight vehicles. Work on the larger vessel, the *Normandie*, continued for delivery in May 1992.

During the late summer three old favourites of the fleet completed their final passenger sailings with Brittany Ferries. The first to stand down was the *Corbière* on 22nd September, followed a week later by the *Trégastel* and lastly the *Reine Mathilde*. The *Corbière* was duly handed back to her owners for further service in the Baltic. The *Trégastel* was sold to P&O Scottish Ferries for their service between Aberdeen (Scotland) and the Shetland and Orkney Isles. Following an extensive refit in Germany the vessel emerged as the *St. Clair* for her new role. The *Reine Mathilde*, which had been sold the previous

Above: The Bretagne *on her first visit to Plymouth.*

Below: Officers on board the Bretagne *during her first season.*

The Barfleur.

BARFLEUR
Votre numéro / your number / su numero :
- PONT / DECK / CUBIERTA
- PORTE OU ESCALIER
  DOOR OR STAIR
  PUERTA O ESCALERA

Accès aux garages
Access to garages
Acceso a los garajes

Truckline

year to an American company, was sent to Brest to be handed over to her new owners. The former *Prince of Brittany* did not leave European waters as originally planned, but was instead to be chartered by her new owners to BCIF for their passenger operations for two years in place of the *Rozel*. Following certain modifications for her new role, she was renamed *Beauport*.

In March 1992 the company announced that it had purchased the German ferry *Nils Holgersson* from TT-Line for £70 million for its Spanish operations. The vessel would undergo a major rebuilding programme and overhaul to make her more suitable for the Spanish route. On her entry into service in 1993, the *Bretagne* would then be transferred to the St.Malo–Portsmouth route, in place of the *Armorique* and the *Duchesse Anne*.

On 4th April the *Barfleur* sailed into Poole from Cherbourg for the first time, her arrival marking the largest ferry ever to dock at the Dorset port where the Harbour Commissioners had carried out a substantial programme of dredging of the main channel pending this historic day. The eight-deck ship, with a capacity for 1,304 passengers and 600 cars or a combination of 304 cars and 66 freight vehicles, offered new standards for the four-hour link. On board, passenger accommodation was designed on Decks 5, 6 and 7, where a wide range of public areas was provided including two restaurants, duty-free shops and boutiques, children's playroom and nursery and a bar.

A month later, Brittany Ferries' second new superferry left Masa Yards in Finland. The new vessel was a far cry from the early days of the company, boasting 220 luxury cabins and a capacity for 2,120 passengers with space for 630 cars on three decks. The elegant interior of the superferry was designed to cruise-like standards, with the main accommodation situated over five decks. On board the *Normandie*, her stylish passenger areas included two cinemas, a duty-free shopping mall, Le Derby bar, the Riva-Bella self-service restaurant, the Deauville à la carte restaurant and terrace bar, the Pays d'Auge tea shop and a most elegant reception area for passengers arriving on board. Original paintings by a selection of artists from Normandy graced the vessel's air-conditioned interior. With an impressive length of 161 metres and a beam of 26 metres, the vessel set new standards for the 'nineties' on the English Channel, as had the *Duc de Normandie* in 1986 when she opened the Caen link.

On Monday 16th May 1992, under the command of Captain Bertrand Apperry, the *Normandie* entered commercial operations between Caen and Portsmouth on the 08.00 sailing to Britain. Her entry into service increased the capacity on the route by some 40% overnight. Following the giant ferry slotting into the timetable, the *Armorique* was transferred to the St. Malo–Portsmouth link for what was going to be her last season on the route, prior to the arrival there of the *Bretagne* the next year.

Further expansion plans were announced by the company in the autumn, with increased sailings between Roscoff and Plymouth for 1993, and additional sailings between Roscoff and Cork would

be introduced to meet the growing demand on the route. In addition to the increased sailings to Ireland, the *Duchesse Anne* would open a new 18-hour route between St. Malo and Cork from mid June.

On 28th January 1993 the *Bretagne* made her debut on the Caen–Portsmouth service and on her arrival the next morning she opened the new seasonal Portsmouth–Santander service, which would operate until March and again from November through the winter. Meanwhile, during the same month, Brittany Ferries took delivery of the *Nils Holgersson* from TT-Line. The former German vessel sailed from Lübeck on 15th January 1993 under her new name *Val de Loire* for Italy, for the major refit and rebuilding programme to equip her for the Spanish and Irish operations.

The major investment, not only in new tonnage but in extensive staff training, was to pay handsome dividends for the company during 1993, when the AA awarded Brittany Ferries a five-star rating for

The Normandie *at Ouistreham (Caen) with the* Normandie Shipper *behind her.*

the *Normandie* and *Bretagne*, making it the only company to receive the highest accolade for ferries operating on the Channel. The other new superferry of the fleet, the *Barfleur*, also won praise for her onboard service, winning four out of the six awards for her self-service restaurant.

Meanwhile, in early 1993 P&O European Ferries, Brittany Ferries' competitors on the Western Channel, announced that they would open a rival service to that of the French company between the UK and Spain.

The new route opened with the chartered *Pride of Bilbao* on 28th April, some two months prior to the entry into service of the company's new *Val de Loire* on the Santander route. The then Managing Director of Brittany Ferries in the UK & Ireland, Ian Carruthers, expressed his concerns for the marketplace to absorb the new capacity between the UK and the Iberian Peninsula. In the event both services to Spain were to expand the market and did not threaten the established operations of Brittany Ferries.

Below: The impressive Val de Loire.

Opposite page: The historical Bretagne *in St. Malo.*

On 18th March the *Duchesse Anne* opened the St. Malo route prior to the transfer of the *Bretagne* from Roscoff later in the year. On the arrival of the *Bretagne* on the St. Malo–Portsmouth route the *Duchesse Anne* was earmarked to offer additional sailings from Roscoff to Cork and to open a new service in her weekly roster between St. Malo and Cork from 21st June. The *Duchesse Anne*'s roster allowed the vessel to sail from Roscoff on a Sunday evening at 18.00 for Cork.

In late May, the company took delivery of its new flagship *Val de Loire*, under the command of Captain Christian Selosse. She sailed to Santander for berthing trials on 2nd June, before sailing to Plymouth on a private cruise for the travel trade and VIPs. The new giant cruise ferry, with capacity for 2,120 passengers and 570 cars or 100 freight vehicles, heralded the climax of the three-year £350 million investment plan which placed the company in the position of operating the youngest fleet on the Channel.

On 9th June 1993 the new flagship of the company entered commercial operations between Plymouth and Santander. Some four days later she reached the Irish port of Cork, making shipping history as the biggest ferry ever to operate from Ireland. Following the *Val de Loire* entering service, the *Bretagne* transferred to the St. Malo route on 14th June, and the *Duchesse Anne* opened the new Cork–St. Malo service on 22nd June.

On 18th December 1993 the *Armorique* was sold to Chinese interests and renamed *Min Nan*.

Brittany Ferries was to see a four-fold increase on its St. Malo route following the introduction of the *Bretagne* to the link. In the light of the success of the service the *Duchesse Anne* was to join the *Bretagne* for the 1994 season from 16th May on a new route from St. Malo to Poole.

The 1994 season was to be a trouble-free year for the company with its ships. The *Val de Loire* at

the end of the summer season was transferred to the Caen route, as in the previous year, to operate in tandem with the *Normandie*. The *Bretagne* meanwhile continued to operate both the Santander and St. Malo routes during the winter from Portsmouth.

1996 was to see the opening of the Channel Tunnel and this was immediately to affect operations in the Western Channel. The company had to re-structure its fares to remain competitive against the ferry operations on the Dover Strait and with the Channel Tunnel. Later in the year the company had to be re-structured in the light of losses caused by continued pressure on fares from the Dover Strait. In France and the UK some staff were made redundant and the freight vessel *Normandie Shipper* was immediately placed on the sale list; the *Duchesse Anne* in spite of her having a successful season on the St. Malo to Cork service was also to be sold.

Meanwhile, Brittany Ferries entered talks with P&O European Ferries with regard to the possible merger of its operations on the Western Channel. In the event both companies decided not to join forces. In spite of the opening of the Channel Tunnel, fortunes on the Western Channel were to improve during the latter part of 1996 with a stronger pound against the French franc. By early March 1997

Brittany Ferries claimed that bookings were up by some 15% from the previous year. By the end of the summer the company was confident that bookings overall were up by some 60% compared with the previous season.

In a surprise move Brittany Ferries announced that the *Barfleur* would be employed on the Spanish service for the forthcoming winter between 28th November and 15th March, instead of the *Bretagne* as in the previous year. The Santander route would be operated from Poole on a 28-hour schedule between both ports. The *Barfleur*'s passenger certificate was reduced to 200 passengers while maintaining the Spanish service. At the time Brittany Ferries claimed that the *Barfleur* had been introduced to analyse whether or not freight traffic could be increased on the route during the winter period in the light of lorry restrictions imposed in France at weekends. The *Barfleur* sailed from Poole for Santander on Fridays at 18.30 with a return sailing from Santander on Sundays at 12.00. For the rest of the week she was rostered on her normal service between Poole and Cherbourg. While the *Barfleur* underwent her refit at Christmas the *Bretagne* was employed in her place but operated from Portsmouth.

Brittany Ferries decided to undertake further reorganisation of the group at the end of 1998, to abandon the Truckline Ferries branding on its Poole–Cherbourg route from 1999 and to bring the Poole services under the branding of the company.

In 1999 the European Union implemented the ending of duty-free, which was to place further pressure on the company's operating profits and similarly those of its rivals on the English Channel.

In a further move to attract business to the Western Channel, Brittany Ferries launched a revolutionary tariff policy for passengers and cars. For the first time, in its brochure for 2000, no tariffs were quoted and potential customers were invited to telephone the company to obtain rates for their travel on similar lines to those of airlines like easyJet. This yield management-type organisation of fares was of course to move onto total yield management control of all fares using the worldwide web. During 1999, with a fleet of seven ships and six routes, the company conveyed 2,654,157 passengers, 690,891 cars and 172,291 freight units, giving the company a 52.2% share of the Western Channel passenger market.

In early 2000, Brittany Ferries announced firm plans to build the first new tonnage for the company since the introduction of the *Normandie*. The new vessel was to be constructed for the successful Caen route and would have capacity for 120 trucks, 600 cars and 2,000 passengers; at the time she would be the largest ship ever built for cross-Channel operations, at a cost of £80 million. The announcement of the new ship followed another year of substantially improved financial results with turnover overall in the group increasing by some 4.1% to £195 million, despite the loss of duty-free.

After fierce competition between three European yards, Brittany Ferries announced on 11th September that it had placed an order to build the new ferry for the Caen service with Van der Giessen-de Noord. On the entry into service of the new ship during 2002, she would displace the *Duc de Normandie*, which would then be transferred to the Roscoff–Plymouth service in place of the *Quiberon*, which would be disposed of. The new state-of-the-art vessel would allow Brittany Ferries to consolidate its position as the number-one operator for both passengers and freight on the Western Channel.

During the same month Brittany Ferries announced that it planned to co-operate with Condor on a joint venture for a new high-speed ferry service between Poole and Cherbourg with the *Condor Vitesse* in 2001. The new fast ferry service would run in tandem with the conventional ferry *Barfleur*. The Condor-owned craft would be painted in the joint livery of Brittany Ferries and Condor.

The keel of the new Brittany Ferries vessel *Mont St Michel* for the Caen route was laid in March with a planned entry into service in May the following year.

The joint fast ferry service between Poole and Cherbourg commenced on 22nd May, ran until the end of September and was to prove an overwhelming success.

During 2001 Brittany Ferries was to see further increases in traffic on its routes, carrying over 2.5 million passengers, an increase of some 1.4% over the previous trading year.

On 15th March 2002 at 07.00 the *Mont St Michel* was launched at the yard of Van der Giessen-de Noord. Sadly the ship had been delayed due to a number of factors and it was anticipated at the time of her launch that she would enter service in late July. Continued delays with the construction of the vessel saw the company not being able to take delivery of her until December.

The Mont St Michel *being launched on 15th March 2002.*

The Mont St Michel.

Enter the cruise ferry era

On 5th June 2002, Brittany Ferries announced plans to build one of the first northern European car ferry to feature such cruise facilities as an indoor swimming pool and cabins with either balcony or terrace, to be introduced on its Spanish service from spring 2004. The new vessel, to be named *Pont-Aven* after the town in western Brittany, would replace the *Val de Loire* on the Spanish, French and Irish routes. Brittany Ferries confirmed in the summer that the new £100 million, 40,000-ton vessel would be built at the German shipyard of Meyer Werft. The *Pont-Aven* when constructed would have a length of 185 metres with a 31-metre beam and would be able to accommodate 2,200 passengers, 650 cars and 20 lorries. With a service speed of 27 knots she would be able to operate the then 24-hour crossing between Plymouth and Santander within 18 hours.

The *Mont St Michel* eventually entered service between Caen and Portsmouth on 20th December. Her arrival at last addressed the imbalance of operations on the Caen route since the delivery of the *Normandie* in 1992.

The *Quiberon* meanwhile completed her last sailing with the company between Portsmouth and Caen on the 09.00 sailing on 20th December. The faithful *Quiberon*, which had operated with the company for 21 years, had seen service on all the company's routes during her career. She was later sold

Views of the Pont-Aven *under construction in Germany.*

to Euro Med Ferries and was subsequently renamed *Guilia d'Abundo* for a new role between Sète and Palma de Mallorca, Ibiza and Menorca.

The *Pont-Aven* left Meyer's shipyard in Germany in the early hours of Saturday 7th February 2004 to allow her to make her passage down the River Ems to the North Sea. The weather conditions were very poor on the day, so much so that the high winds and sleet on her passage delayed her at the entrance to the Ems barrier for about an hour. After reaching the open water, she then made her way to Eemshaven (Holland) for her final fitting-out and trials at sea.

The *Pont-Aven*, the seventh vessel to be built for Brittany Ferries, was handed over by the German shipbuilders three days ahead of her scheduled delivery date on 27th February. She then made her

The completed Pont-Aven arriving at Plymouth for the first time.

way down the English Channel to Roscoff via Caen, arriving at the Breton port on 2nd March for berthing trials and then a near three-week period of further fitting-out and settling down by her crew prior to her entry into service.

The *Pont-Aven* then made her maiden voyage to Spain on the morning of 24th March; she had made her first commercial sailing prior to that at 23.15 the night before between Roscoff and Plymouth. During April she undertook a series of special press trips in Ireland, UK, France and Spain. The Plymouth–Santander roster for 2004 initially allowed for sailings on Sundays and Wednesdays from Plymouth at 12.00 with arrival times in Spain at 13.00. Departures from Spain were then Mondays and Thursdays with a 23-hour crossing back to the

UK. This allowed the *Pont-Aven* to settle down on the route before commencing her faster operations from 4th April. Her schedules from that date allowed for departures on Sundays and Wednesdays from Plymouth at 16.00 with arrivals at Santander at 11.00. Return crossings were offered during her first season on Mondays and Thursdays from Spain, leaving at 16.00 with arrival the next morning at Plymouth at 09.00. During the main summer period she was re-scheduled to leave Plymouth on Sundays at 20.00 and Wednesdays at 13.00 with return sailings on Mondays and Thursdays at 18.00 and 14.00 respectively.

For the first time Brittany Ferries was to see competition on its Portsmouth–Caen service from P&O Ferries with the fast ferry service operated by the British company. The competition was to be short-lived, only for one season, and made very little difference to Brittany Ferries' operations as the rival service created its own market.

For 2004 Brittany Ferries opened a new service between Portsmouth and Cherbourg from 5th April using the *Val de Loire* on Mondays, Tuesdays, Wednesdays and Thursdays and during the peak season the operation was covered by the *Bretagne* on Mondays to Thursdays. The schedule offered proved to be less than inviting to the travelling public and was to damage its existing and successful St. Malo operation. The link attracted very little traffic.

In September P&O Ferries announced rationalisation plans throughout their ferry operations in the UK. As part of these plans the company stated that they would close their Portsmouth–Cherbourg route and proposed to hand over their rival Le Havre service to Brittany Ferries, together with their ships the *Pride of Portsmouth* and *Pride of Le Havre*, which would be renamed *Etretat* and *Honfleur*. The Office of Fair Trading (OFT) in the UK investigated the proposed takeover of the Le Havre service and decided

not to give the 'green light' to P&O's proposals. The decision of the OFT was regretted by all parties.

Brittany Ferries decided to withdraw from the proposed agreement following the decision of the OFT. In a statement in March Brittany Ferries said that during the five ensuing months market trends in both volume and revenue yield had led the Board to conclude it would not be commercially sound to continue with the transaction; the company instead would now concentrate on developing its existing routes to France. Eventually P&O Ferries announced they would close their Le Havre route in September 2005.

With the withdrawal of P&O's operations between Portsmouth and Cherbourg, Brittany Ferries quickly established the service with the *Normandie* on 2nd January and thereafter the *Val de Loire*. Meanwhile, Brittany Ferries announced that its Portsmouth–Cherbourg route for the summer would be operated by the newly acquired fast craft *Normandie Express*, which would have capacity for 900 passengers and 280 cars. She would be employed on two round sailings a day between Portsmouth and Cherbourg, apart from Fridays, Saturdays and Sundays when she would provide additional capacity on the Caen route. The service would operate until 10th November and would be based in Portsmouth with both French and British crews. The *Normandie Express* was constructed by the Australian company InCat and was able to achieve a service speed of 42 knots. She had started her career as the *Lynx* for TranzRail in New Zealand between Wellington and Picton. On the arrival of the *Normandie Express* the *Val de Loire* transferred to the St. Malo route as the mainstay of the service, while the *Bretagne* was transferred to the Roscoff–Plymouth route in place of the *Duc de Normandie* following her disposal earlier in the year.

The *Normandie Express* arrived in France on 22nd February on her delivery voyage from New Zealand. The new fast craft operation was to have a trouble-free season and was to achieve good loadings on both the Cherbourg and Caen routes. The winter roster of the Cherbourg route was covered by the *Val de Loire* following the completion of the *Normandie Express'* season on the route.

During August 2005 Brittany Ferries announced it had entered into an agreement with Aker Yards in Finland to build a new ro-ro vessel for the Cherbourg–Poole service to replace the ageing *Coutances*. The new ship for delivery in 2007 would have a capacity of 2,200 lane metres and 120 cabins. Meanwhile on 30th September P&O Ferries closed their Le Havre route and in a surprise move LD Lines re-established the service using one vessel on the link instead of P&O's previous two ferries.

On 25th November Brittany Ferries announced that it had sold the *Val de Loire* to DFDS Seaways and taken a medium-term charter from the Danish company of the *Dana Anglia*. The chartered ship would be renamed *Pont l'Abbé* and would be placed on the Plymouth–Roscoff service in place of the *Bretagne* which would return to her former route between St. Malo and Portsmouth. In the light of the disposal of the *Val de Loire* the company announced plans to build a new vessel for the Plymouth–Roscoff service at Aker Yards in Finland for 2009. The new ship would be modelled on the *Mont St Michel* and would be built specifically for the passenger and freight requirements between Brittany and the West Country. The *Pont l'Abbé* would continue on the Roscoff service until her delivery.

During 2005 Brittany Ferries increased passenger and freight carryings largely due to the demise of P&O Ferries' operations from Portsmouth. Passenger numbers rose by 8.8% to 2.46 million and freight

increased by a dramatic 10.1% to 232,723 units.

The *Val de Loire* completed her last commercial sailing between Portsmouth and Cherbourg on 20th February 2006. The repainted and chartered *Pont l'Abbé* entered Brittany Ferries' service between Portsmouth and Cherbourg on 6th March prior to transferring to the Roscoff route on 31st March. In November Brittany Ferries announced that its new ship for its Roscoff–Plymouth service would be named *Armorique*. The naming of the new ship was a nice touch by the company following the previous vessel of the same name's distinguished career. On 29th November the keel of the *Cotentin*, the new freight vessel for the Cherbourg–Poole service, was laid.

After 30 years of service between Cherbourg and Poole the *Coutances* completed her final sailing on 26th April 2008. During her career on the English Channel she carried out more than 36,000 crossings. In August the new luxury cruise ferry the *Armorique* was launched in Finland. The vessel made her first commercial sailing the following February from Plymouth, during the out of season periods in the future she would cover the operations of the company during refits.

During December 2009 Brittany Ferries announced that it had acquired the German-built vessel *Superfast V* from her Greek operators Superfast. Built in a very successful series of twelve vessels for Attica Enterprises S.A, the new ship boosted capacity on the Portsmouth–Santander route twice a week initially and additional sailings from Portsmouth to Cherbourg. The former Greek ship offered capacity for 1,600 passengers, 712 cars/77 lorries. She left Greece on 16th February renamed as the *Cap Finistère* and then undertook berthing trials at Cherbourg and Portsmouth on 22/23rd February, before sailing to Dunkerque for a major refit. A month later she entered commercial operations from Cherbourg to Portsmouth.

The **Armorique** in 2016, shortly after her scrubber conversion.

As the *Cap Finistère* entered service on the English Channel, the *Barfleur* was withdrawn from operations and laid up for sale or long-term charter work.

In April 2010 all flights in and out of the UK and several other European countries where suspended following ash from a volcanic eruption in Iceland. Up to 4,000 flights were cancelled with airspace closed in Britain, Ireland, Northern France, Norway, Sweden, Finland and Denmark among others. During the volcanic ash incident, Brittany Ferries carried over 35,000 additional passengers to that of the previous year, following passengers having to make their over-Europe-by-land transport to Spanish and French ferry ports.

Following P&O Ferries' withdrawal of the ferry operations to Bilbao, Brittany Ferries announced its own plans to open a route to the city using the *Cap Finistère* twice a week from Portsmouth. The company was now offering five sailings a week between the UK and Spain.

The *Barfleur* returned to operations again on the Cherbourg–Poole service until September 2011, when the service was withdrawn again; she was then chartered to DFDS the following year to operate on the Dover–Calais service as the *Deal Seaways* for six

months. Following this period on the Dover Strait she returned to operations on the Cherbourg link to Poole the next March.

In spite of strong passenger numbers and sterling being strong against the euro, Brittany Ferries had to undertake a series of cutbacks within its operations for the following season, with continued losses.

Brittany Ferries celebrated its 40th anniversary on 3rd January 2013. The planned celebrations were reduced in the light of cutbacks announced during October the year before, including a visit of the *Pont-Aven* to the Thames and Greenwich. In spite of the losses in the company, it was announced that *Normandie Express* would open a new ferry route between Le Havre and Portsmouth as from 16th May.

With the continued high operating costs of the *Cotentin*, the freight-only vessel was withdrawn from operations between France and Spain. She made her last commercial sailing on 30th September 2013 from

The Baie de Seine.

Santander to Poole. She was later chartered on a long-term basis to Stena Line for operations in the Baltic.

Brittany Ferries' Economie

With the increased popularity of cheap no-frills airlines like Ryanair and easyJet, Brittany Ferries embarked on similar operations of its own with a 'no frills' operation between Le Havre–Portsmouth and Portsmouth–Santander with a charter of ro-pax vessel *Etretat* from Stena RoRo. Marketed under Brittany Ferries' Economie, the *Etretat* entered service in May. In spite of a very different operation to the rest of the fleet, both services proved very popular with fares starting at £169 one-way for a car with two passengers between the UK and Spain.

During September the company reported a record year for carryings, with almost three quarters of a million passengers using its operations from Portsmouth to France and Spain, a dramatic turnaround overall including that of the new 'Economie' operations.

The company had been considering converting the *Mont St Michel, Pont-Aven* and *Armorique* to LNG in the light of the new emission controls coming into force in 2015. The other vessels in the fleet, apart from the *Bretagne* would have scrubbers fitted to meet the new regulations. In the event, in November the company decided not to convert the three ships to LNG for a number of factors and also not to build a purpose-built LNG-powered ship codenamed PEGASIS (Power Efficient GAS Innovative Ship) for the Spanish routes. The *Mont St Michel, Pont-Aven* and *Armorique* burned diesel oil for the next season until their conversion during the winter of 2015/2016.

The *Normandie* was the first ship to undergo conversion, appearing in early January with a new funnel housing part of the scrubber system. The *Cap Finistère* followed and then the *Barfleur* in early 2015.

In January 2015 Brittany Ferries announced that it had chartered the former *Dana Sirena* from DFDS for a five-year period to replace the *Etretat* on the Spanish service and to further expand the operations on the both Bilbao and Santander services. The vessel was renamed the *Baie de Seine* and like the *Etretat* she was branded under the 'économie'. While the facilities on board were of a very high standard, the company felt the ship did not quite meet the criteria of the other ships on the Spanish service and with her slower service speed than her counterparts, it was felt that she met the 'économie' operation better. The *Baie de Seine* entered commercial operations on 7th May on a special sailing from Cherbourg to Portsmouth. Two days later she undertook her first sailing to Spain. On entry into service of the *Baie de Seine*, the *Etretat* increased her sailings on the Le Havre–Portsmouth route.

During 2015, Brittany Ferries operated ten routes and over 142 weekly sailings during the peak period with a fleet of ten ships.

In September the *Mont St Michel* sailed to Spain to undergo her scrubber conversion; she was later followed by the *Armorique* and *Pont-Aven*, who where sent to Poland for their conversion work.

Further expansion plans were announced in January to offer more freight capacity between Spain and the UK, with the chartered French freight vessel *Pelican* to open a new freight-only operation between Poole and Bilbao. With a capacity for 100 units it not only expanded the company's operations but also allowed additional capacity for cars on the passenger ships. During 2015 the company had reported a 20% increase in freight traffic across all routes. The *Pelican* took operations up on 11th February 2016.

In June the company celebrated 30 years of operations between Caen and Portsmouth. In spite of Brexit, Brittany Ferries showed again another

significant increase in passengers and cars on all its routes with some 392,446 passengers travelling with the company in the August on all its operations, a 4.4% increase on that of the previous year. The company recorded a record day on 14th August, when 21,900 passengers were carried.

The Mont St Michel *and* Cap Finistère *after their scrubber conversion.*

Above: The Galicia *under construction at the AVIC shipyard in Weihai, China.*

Below: The Cap Finistère *with the new Brittany Ferries logo and livery introduced in November 2018.*

Four new ships

On 21st December, Brittany Ferries signed a letter of intent with Flensburger Schiffbau-Gesellschaft Shipyard in Germany for the construction of a new ship powered by LNG for its Caen link. The new ferry would enter service in summer 2019 in place of the *Normandie*, which would then go on the Le Havre link.

Both the *Barfleur* and *Normandie* celebrated their 25 years of service on the English Channel. In spite of their age and valiant service, both ships have aged little due to their advanced profile designs when they came in to service in 1992 and the continued investment by the company to keep them well maintained. During the 25 years of service of the *Normandie*, she had carried over 13 million passengers, 7 million cars, 2.5 million freight units and covered over 5 million nautical miles on her 51,000 crossings between Caen and Portsmouth.

Brittany Ferries confirmed the construction of its new ferry in June at a special press conference in the picturesque town of Honfleur. The new LNG powered ship will be named the *Honfleur*, following a long tradition of the company naming ships after beautiful destinations in France. Brittany Ferries claimed at the time that the new ferry would be the most environmentally friendly ship operating in UK waters when she enters service in 2020 on the Caen–Portsmouth service.

The *Honfleur* will carry up to 1,680 passengers and will offer 257 cabins, two cinemas, restaurants, boutique shopping and expansive passenger lounges. She will operate alongside Brittany Ferries' *Mont St Michel* on three daily return sailings.

To address the issues of LNG infrastructure, specifically the lack of storage facilities in ports served by its ships, Brittany Ferries has partnered with Total for an innovative delivery solution in

France. The *Honfleur* will be the first passenger ship in the world to be equipped with on-board cranes that allow 40 feet LNG containers to be lifted into a fixed position. The containers will be transported by truck from an LNG terminal at Dunkirk and then driven on board. They will then be hoisted into position alongside a fixed 'mother' LNG storage tank located at the rear of the superstructure. On her next call at port, empty containers will be removed and replenished with full units.

On 25th May 2018, Brittany Ferries confirmed the charter of two brand new cruiseferries to serve its services from the UK to Spain, to be named *Galicia* and *Salamanca*. The 927-passenger ships will be tailored to Brittany Ferries' needs and will receive extra cabins, although the 3,100 lane metre capacity will be retained. Both ships will be built at the Avic International Weihai shipyard in China, with the first arriving in November 2021.

In March 2019 the company confirmed the charter of a third 'E Flexer' vessel from China. In July Brittany Ferries confirmed that the new ship would be named *Santoña* continuing the theme of naming the new ships after Spanish towns and regions of northern Iberia.

This first ship will replace the *Baie de Seine,* which will be returned to her owners DFDS. The second ship is due arrive during 2022 and will replace the *Cap Finistère*, which will either be put on the Irish routes or sold. Both ships, together with the *Honfleur*, will spearhead a wide-ranging, five-year fleet-renewal and modernisation programme worth around £400m.

The new ships are being chartered from the Swedish shipping company Stena RoRo, as part of its new generation of state-of-the-art 'E-Flexer' vessels. Measuring some 42,400 tonnes and 215 metres long, the new vessels will be the longest in Brittany Ferries' fleet. Their impressive dimensions will allow

A view of the Honfleur *being built at the FSG shipyard in Germany, taken in September 2019.*

them to carry almost two miles of freight vehicles apiece. This will be also the first time that the company has ever operated sister ships in its fleet in its 45 year history. Portsmouth will serve as the base for both ferries.

During 2017 the company operated 844 sailings on routes from Portsmouth, Poole and Plymouth to Santander (Cantabria) and Bilbao (Basque Country), carrying 331,000 passengers and 150,000 cars. That was around 80% more than ten years earlier. During 2017, Brittany Ferries carried around 40,000 freight units between the UK and Spain.

It is not clear as to the future of the *Pont-Aven* after 2022, she may remain on the Spanish link after the arrival of the *Galicia*, *Salamanca* and *Santoña*, it all depends as to whether the 'Bretagne II' project proceeds in the near future to replace the much loved *Bretagne* which will be 33 years old by the time the three new ships from China enter service.

Quelques mots en français

Ci-dessus : Les routes desservies par Brittany Ferries en 2019.

A droite : Le Quiberon *croise le* Trégastel *dans la Manche dans les années 80.*

La Brittany Ferries a débuté modestement en 1973 comme compagnie maritime de transport de marchandises destinée à favoriser l'exportation vers la Grande-Bretagne de la production des coopératives agricoles bretonnes. Aujourd'hui, elle exploite une flotte de ferries modernes offrant des liaisons inégalées sur la Manche occidentale entre la Grande-Bretagne, la France et l'Irlande, de même que sur le Golfe de Gascogne vers l'Espagne. La compagnie bretonne est passée d'un navire unique (le *Kerisnel*) à une flotte moderne composée d'une douzaine de navires transportant plus d'un million de passagers par an partant de onze ports.

La ligne la plus populaire reste celle de Portsmouth-Caen/Ouistreham,

qui transporte environ 30% du trafic passagers. Cette route ouverte en 1986 aura vu sa capacité encore augmentée en 2020 grâce à l'introduction du *Honfleur*, premier bâtiment de la compagnie propulsé au GNL et l'un des ferries les plus respectueux de l'environnement opérant sur la Manche.

Brittany Ferries poursuit sa croissance sur ses routes irlandaises et espagnoles, ayant notamment ouvert en 2018 la première liaison directe par ferry entre l'Irlande et l'Espagne. D'ici 2023, la société aura investi environ 550 millions d'euros dans quatre nouveaux navires : le *Honfleur*, et les sister-ships *Galicia*, *Salamanca* et *Santoña*.

La société est aujourd'hui l'un des principaux acteurs régionaux français sur le plan économique et social : 81% de ses activités d'achats, de stockage et de maintenance profitent à la Bretagne, à la Normandie, aux Pays de la Loire et à l'Ile de France, et elle emploie 2 500 personnes – dont 1 700 de personnel navigant – qui eux-mêmes contribuent indirectement à 4 500 emplois supplémentaires.

Précisions concernant les descriptions de bateaux (pages 44 à 87) :

L'année mentionnée à côté du nom du bateau est celle de son entrée en service chez Brittany Ferries.

Spécifications techniques :
Chantier naval + année de construction / Jauge brute (g = tjb) / Longueur hors tout x largeur hors tout / Propulsion / Vitesse de croisière.

Capacité passagers / Capacité voitures / Capacité fret (si connue) / Capacité garage en mètres (si connue).

Années de service chez Brittany Ferries (sauf pour les navires toujours en service fin 2019).

Kerisnel – 1973

The *Kerisnel* was built in Vigo in Spain. Alexis Gourvennec, who at this time was the chairman of the SICA of Saint-Pol-de-Léon, convinced its farmer members to fund the purchase of this ship, which would be able to export their vegetables to England. They bought the vessel in November 1972 for Fr5 million; the other

ROSCOFF
PLYMOUTH
par le car-ferry "kerisnel"

BRETAGNE
ANGLETERRE
IRLANDE

Fr10 million were funded by the Crédit Agricole. Following a short charter to P&O Normandy Ferries, the vessel arrived in Roscoff on 20th December 1972 to perform her first trials and she was then renamed *Kerisnel*.

She undertook her maiden crossing on 3rd January 1973. Such was the success of the new operation that in October 1974 she was sold in the light of larger tonnage, with more passenger accommodation being required.

Astilleros & Construcciones S.A, Vigo, Spain, 1972
3,395g / 99.2 x 16.6 m / Single screw / 16 knots
12 pass. / 540 lane metres
Brittany Ferries service: 1972-1974

Above: Alexis Gourvennec.

Left: Roscoff port pictured in the early stages of construction.

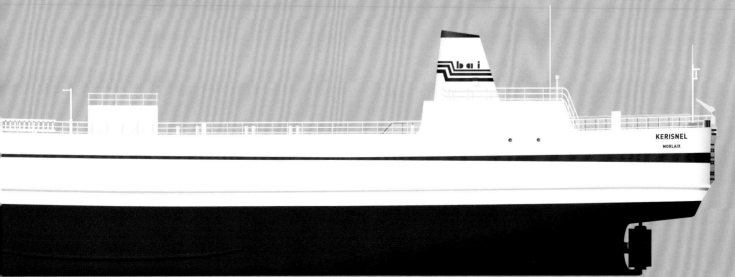

Penn Ar Bed - 1974

The *Penn Ar Bed* was ordered by Bretagne Angleterre Irlande SA in late 1972, shortly after the company was established. She was launched on 17th May 1973 and was delivered to BAI in January 1974, replacing *Kerisnel*. She made her maiden voyage on 24th January between Roscoff and Plymouth. *Penn Ar Bed*'s name comes from the Breton translation of Finistère, meaning the Land's End.

The introduction of *Penn Ar Bed* enabled the company to carry more passengers, although her capacity of only 250 passengers soon appeared to be too small to cope with the growing passenger traffic. In August 1975, the *Penn Ar Bed* was transferred to the St Malo–Plymouth/Portsmouth service, replacing the *Prince de Bretagne*. The St Malo service was created to secure Brittany Ferries' access to the new French port after the attempt of TT-Line in establishing a service from Southampton to St Malo.

The service was repeated the following year but, with larger tonnage coming on stream in Brittany Ferries, she was used less and less in operations. Some six years later the *Penn Ar Bed* was sold to Rolf Erikson and renamed *Sveno Marina*.

Société Nouvelle des Ateliers & Chantiers de la Rochelle-Pallice, France, 1974
2,891g / 103.9 x 17.5 m / Twin screw / 18.5 knots
250 pass. / 235 cars
Brittany Ferries service: 1974-1984

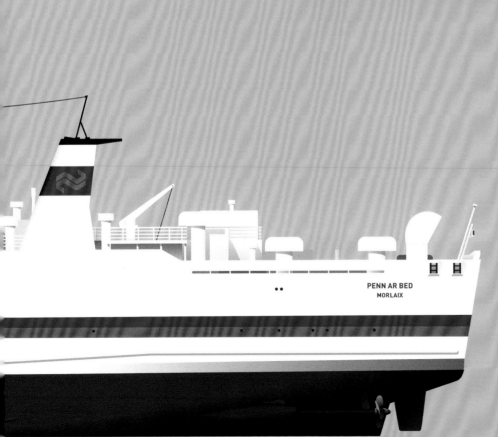

PENN AR BED
MORLAIX

Prince de Bretagne - 1975 (chartered)

Trondheims Mekaniske Verksted, Trondheim, Norway, 1975
2,424g / 109.7 x 16.5 m / Twin screw / 19 knots
346 pass. / 250 cars
Brittany Ferries service: 1975

Built as the Falster for operations in the Baltic, this freight ship was chartered by Brittany Ferries in 1975 for the Roscoff service. With a passenger certificate for only 345 the vessel was unsuitable for the growing traffic with Brittany Ferries.

Armorique - 1976

The *Armorique* was built at Le Havre in France. She was launched on 24th April 1971 as *Terje Vigen*. She was delivered to DA-NO Linien on 13th May 1972 for services between Oslo and Åarhus. After only three years' service in Scandinavia, she was sold to Brittany Ferries in 1975 and renamed *Armorique*. She entered service in 1976 on the Roscoff–Plymouth route, was then transferred to the St Malo–Plymouth route in April and a month later, in May, she was operating on the St Malo–Portsmouth link. On 6th July, she ran aground off St Malo in fog and was damaged. She did not return to service until the following year. In

April 1978, she opened the new Plymouth–Santander route.

On the arrival of the *Quiberon*, the *Armorique* became the mainstay of the St Malo–Portsmouth service. From March 1986 she was chartered to SMZ and served on the Harwich–Hoek van Holland route. The next month, she returned to the St Malo route. During her career with Brittany Ferries she held the accolade of serving on all the company's routes, as well operating for Brittany Ferries' sister company British Channel Island Ferries and Truckline.

In December 1990, she was chartered by the French military and sailed from Toulon to Yanbu, Saudi Arabia, via the Suez Canal with 850 troops as part of the First Gulf War. She returned to service on the St Malo–Portsmouth route once again in May.

In December 1993, *Armorique* was sold to the Xiamen Ocean Shipping Company and was renamed *Min Nan*.

Société Nouvelle des Ateliers & Chantiers du Havre, France, 1972
5,732g / 116.6 x 19.2 m / Twin screw / 20 knots
700 pass. / 170 cars
Brittany Ferries service: 1976–1993

ARMORIQUE
MORLAIX

Cornouailles - 1977

The *Cornouailles* was ordered by Brittany Ferries from a Norwegian yard to replace the *Prince de Bretagne* (ex-*Falster*, later *Vega*), which had been delivered by the Norwegian shipyard two years earlier. The *Prince de Bretagne* lacked sufficient passenger accommodation, so a similarly designed ferry was built, but with passenger accommodation for 550.

As passenger traffic continued to grow with Brittany Ferries she was displaced by larger tonnage. In 1984 she was chartered to SNCF for their Dieppe–Newhaven operation, operating alongside the *Chartres* and *Senlac*.

Returning to her owners in January 1986, she initiated a freight-only service on the new Ouistreham–Portsmouth route before being deployed that summer on a new passenger service on the Cherbourg–Poole Truckline operation that Brittany Ferries had acquired the previous year.

This operation proved successful and for 1989 the ship was replaced and transferred to British Channel Island Ferries (BCIF), and renamed the *Havelet*.

There she would begin over a decade of service to the Channel Islands. When BCIF was taken over by rivals Condor in 1994, she operated in a support role for the fast ferry operation; in late 1999 she was laid up for sale. She was eventually sold to Montenegro Lines for their route between Bar and Bari in the Mediterranean.

Trondheims Mekaniske Verksted, Trondheim, Norway, 1977
3,383g / 110 x 16.5 m / Twin screw / 17 knots
550 pass. / 205 cars / 450 lane metres
Brittany Ferries service: 1977-1989

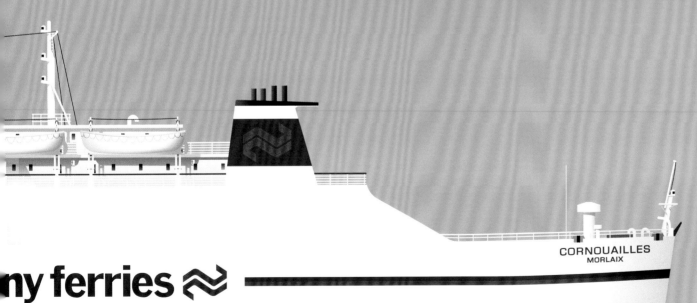

ny ferries

CORNOUAILLES
MORLAIX

Prince Of Brittany - 1978 / Reine Mathilde - 1989

The *Prince of Brittany* was built as the *Prince of Fundy* in 1970 by Schiffbau Gesellschaft Unterweser, AG, in Germany, for the Lion Ferry service between Portland, Maine, and Yarmouth, Nova Scotia. She was to operate the ferry service in Canada between 1970 and 1976. The following year she was moved to the Varberg–Grenå route in Europe until March 1978. She was then chartered to Brittany Ferries from April 1978, initially to sail on the Plymouth–Santander route. Her main role was to be on the Portsmouth–St Malo link and she was renamed *Prince of Brittany*. Eleven years later, she was renamed *Reine Mathilde* in preparation for her transfer to the Portsmouth–Caen (Ouistreham) route to operate alongside the *Duc de Normandie*. Prior to the arrival of the *Normandie* in 1992, she was laid up and sold.

British Channel Island Ferries (BCIF), a sister company of Brittany Ferries, subsequently chartered her. In 1992, she took up service between Poole and the Channel Islands as the *Beauport*. By the end of 1993 BCIF was experiencing

PRINCE OF BRITTANY

financial difficulties due to competition from Condor Ferries and the *Beauport* was returned to her owner, her role within BCIF being taken by the *Havelet*. The *Beauport* was laid up in Southampton until mid-1994 when she was chartered to the Stern Maritime Line for its Bari–Cesme route.

Schiffbau Gessellschaft Unterweser, AG, Bremerhaven, Germany, 1970
5,464g / 119.6 x 18.1 m / Twin screw / 17 knots
1,020 pass. / 210 cars / 20 lorries
Brittany Ferries service: 1978–1989

Goëlo - 1980 (chartered)

A/S Langesund Mekaniske Verksted, Langesund, Norway, 1967
5,073g / 110.8 x 10.8 m / Twin screw / 23.5 knots
1,170 pass. / 210 cars
Brittany Ferries service: 1980-1982

Built for Stena Line as the Stena Britannica in 1967, after only a year of operation between Sweden and Denmark she was sold for service in America. In 1974 she returned to Europe to operate for Viking Line as the Viking 6. In 1980 she was chartered to Brittany Ferries for two years and renamed the Goëlo for the St Malo link.

Breizh-Izel - 1981

Taikoo Dockyard & Eng. Co, Quarry Bay, Hongkong, 1970
2,769g / 111.7 x 17.1 m / Twin screw / 16.5 knots
12 pass. / 65 trailers
Brittany Ferries service: 1980-1987

Built in 1970 as the Wanaka for Union Steamship in New Zealand (Christchurch–Wellington service). Sold to Brittany Ferries in 1980 and renamed the Breizh-Izel. Over the next nine years she was to cover various freight operations for the company, and between 1987 and 1989 she operated for the sister company BCIF. Sold in 1989 for further service in Greece.

Quiberon - 1982

Werft Nobiskrug GmbH, Rendsburg, Germany, 1975
7,927g / 129 x 21.1 m) / Twin screw / 22 knots
1,140 pass. / 252 cars / 540 lane metres
Brittany Ferries service: 1982-2002

Built as the Nils Dacke for the Malmö–Travemünde service. In 1982 she was chartered and then later sold to Brittany Ferries and renamed the Quiberon for the Plymouth/Santander and Cork services; she was displaced by the Bretagne on the Spanish and Irish services. She completed her career on the Caen–Portsmouth link in 2002.

Bénodet - 1983 (chartered) / Corbière - 1985

Jos L. Meyer Werft, Papenburg, Germany, 1970
4,238g / 108.1 x 17.2 m / Twin screw / 18.5 knots
1,200 pass. / 260 cars
Brittany Ferries service: 1983-1985/1989 (BCIF)

Built as the Apollo for Baltic operations, she later operated with Olau Line as the Olau Kent before been sold to Danish owners. In 1983 she was chartered to Brittany Ferries and renamed the Bénodet for the Roscoff–Plymouth service. The following year she was renamed the Corbière and chartered to BCIF, then in 1989 to Truckline for a few months before being sold to Eckerö Line.

Trégastel - 1985

Schiffbau-Gesellschaft Unterweser AG, Bremerhaven, Germany, 1971
3,999g / 118 x 18.5 m / Twin screw / 20.5 knots
1,500 pass. / 370 cars
Brittany Ferries service: 1985-1991

Built as the Travemünde in 1971 for service between Gedser–Travemünde. After a short period as the Njegos, operating between Bari and Bar, she was chartered to Brittany Ferries in place of the Bénodet. After six years service operating under both Brittany Ferries and Truckline brands, she was sold to P&O Scottish Ferries and renamed St Clair.

Duc de Normandie - 1986

The *Duc de Normandie* was built in 1978 as the *Prinses Beatrix* for Stoomvaart Maatschappij Zeeland for their joint Sealink route between Hoek van Holland and Harwich. She was named and launched by HRH Princess Beatrix on 14th January 1978.

Brittany Ferries bought her in October 1985 for the new Caen link. Prior to entering service she underwent a major refit for her new role on the English Channel. She was renamed the *Duc de Normandie* for the new Ouistreham (Caen)–Portsmouth service as from June 1986. The vessel and route proved to be very successful in a very short period and she was later joined by the *Reine Mathilde* prior to the arrival of the new purpose-built *Normandie*.

On the arrival of *Mont St Michel* in July 2002, she was transferred to the Plymouth–Roscoff route, replacing the

Quiberon. She ended her Brittany Ferries career with the company in September 2004. The following year she was sold.

She's still in existence in 2019, named the *Vronskiy* and linking Spain to Morocco.

Verolme Scheepswerf Heusden B.V, Heusden, Holland, 1978
13,505g / 131 x 22.6 m / Twin screw / 21 knots
1,500 pass. / 320 cars / 528 lane metres
Brittany Ferries service: 1986-2005

DUC DE NORMANDIE
CAEN

ries

Duchesse Anne - 1989

The *Duchesse Anne* was built as the *Connacht* for the Cork–Pembroke Dock service for B&I Line. She opened the new link in May 1979 but the service did not attract the traffic, in spite of cutting down the sea passage to Ireland in favour of the west Wales port. After a series of restructuring programmes within the Irish company during the eighties, and with continued heavy operating losses of the state-owned company, she was sold to Brittany Ferries in 1988. The renamed ferry was to spend most of her career with the company operating out of St Malo to Portsmouth, Plymouth and Poole. In 1993 she opened a new route between St Malo and Cork. With larger tonnage coming on stream she was sold in 1996 to Jadrolinija.

Verolme Cork Dockyards Ltd, Cork, Ireland, 1979
9,796g / 122 x 18.8 m / Twin screw / 20 knots
1,500 pass. / 332 cars
Brittany Ferries service: 1989-1996

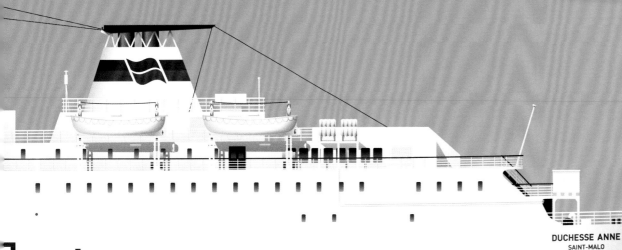

DUCHESSE ANNE
SAINT-MALO

Bretagne - 1989

Built by Chantiers de l'Atlantique for the Plymouth–Santander and Cork–Roscoff services (with two sailings per week between Plymouth and Roscoff), the *Bretagne* was the first 'super ferry' to join the Brittany Ferries fleet and set new standards for ferry design and travel comfort.

The *Bretagne* bears the most symbolic name in the fleet, being the French for 'Brittany' itself, the region of North Western France where the company was started and is still based today. With nearly 30 years' service, the *Bretagne* has become a firm favourite with her passengers. She was originally designed for use on the

Plymouth–Santander and Roscoff–Cork routes to cope with expanding volumes of traffic, but in 1993 she was transferred to the highly popular Portsmouth to St Malo route. In 2004 she also operated between Portsmouth and Cherbourg. In 2005 she operated between Plymouth and Roscoff and in 2006 she returned to the Portsmouth–St Malo route. In early 2009

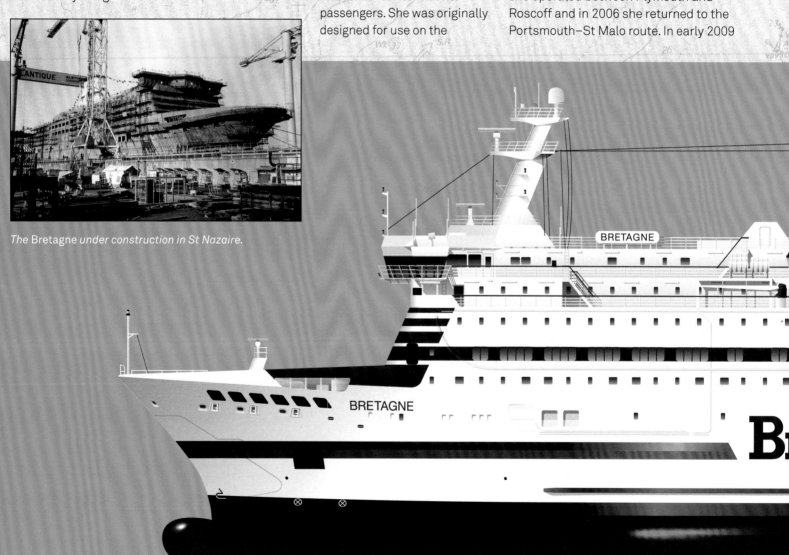

The Bretagne *under construction in St Nazaire.*

the *Bretagne* underwent an extensive £5 million refit to bring her in line with the rest of the fleet, during which Deck 8 was completely re-designed giving it a more modern and contemporary feel.

Chantiers de l'Atlantique, St. Nazaire, France, 1989
24,534g / 151.2 x 26 m / Twin screw / 21 knots
2,056 pass. / 580 cars / 735 lane metres

Normandie - 1992

Following the success of the *Bretagne*, in 1991 Brittany Ferries commissioned a new superferry for the route between Portsmouth and Caen, with a view to significantly increasing the capacity on this link.

Built by Kvaerner Masa-Yards, Turku, Finland, the *Normandie* was delivered to Brittany Ferries in May 1992. The

largest ferry ever to enter the port of Portsmouth, this imposing, 161-metre long new vessel set new standards for the 90's on the English Channel, offering a rather unbalanced service with the *Duc de Normandie* on the Caen route until the arrival of the *Mont St Michel*.

The *Normandie* was fitted with scrubber units in October 2015 and on the arrival of the *Honfleur* in 2020 she will transfer to the Le Havre–Portsmouth link.

Kvaerner Masa-Yards, Turku, Finland, 1992
27,541g / 161 x 26 m / Twin screw / 20.5 knots
2,160 pass. / 648 cars / 1,720 lane metres

TUG

NORMANDIE
CAEN

Val de Loire - 1993

The *Val de Loire* was built as the *Nils Holgersson* for TT-Line's Trelleborg (Sweden) and Travemünde (West Germany) service. She was delivered in February 1987 but was only to remain in the fleet for less than six years. In January 1993 the *Nils Holgersson* was sold to Brittany Ferries and renamed the *Val de Loire*.

Before entering service the ship was rebuilt at La Spezia, Italy with a new streamlined forward superstructure, a refined bow and refurbished interiors based on a maritime feel, with many artefacts and ship models on display in her public areas. The passenger facilities on board *Val de Loire* were very similar in style to those found on board the *Normandie* and *Barfleur*. In 2004 the new *Pont-Aven* replaced the *Val de Loire* on her old routes, and she was transferred to serve on the Portsmouth–St Malo and Portsmouth–Cherbourg routes. In

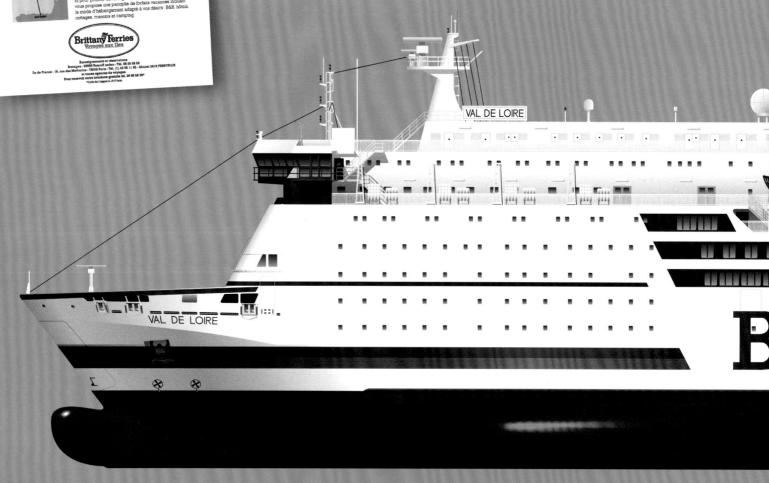

November 2005 she was sold to DFDS Seaways. Her final crossing with Brittany Ferries was between Portsmouth and Cherbourg on 20th February 2006, she was later renamed *King of Scandinavia*.

Schichau Seebeckswerft AG, Bremerhaven, Germany, 1987
31,360g / 161.5 x 32 m / Twin screw / 21 knots
2,280 pass. / 570 cars / 1,250 lane metres
Brittany Ferries service: 1993-2006

VAL DE LOIRE
MORLAIX

Barfleur - 1992 (Truckline) / 1999 (Brittany Ferries)

The *Barfleur* was built by Kvaerner Masa-Yards, Helsinki for Truckline (the freight division of Brittany Ferries) for the Poole–Cherbourg service, to replace two passenger vessels and to inaugurate a year-round passenger service. In 1999 the Truckline branding was dropped for passenger services and she was repainted into full Brittany Ferries livery. In 2005 she operated partly on the Cherbourg–Poole and on the Cherbourg–Portsmouth routes, but in 2006 she returned to operating mainly to Poole.

In February 2010 the *Barfleur* was laid up following the conventional car ferry service ending, and in February 2011 she

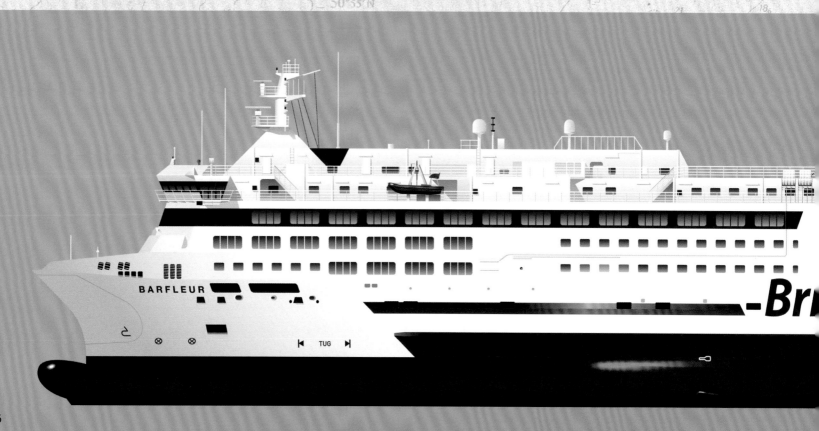

resumed service again on the Poole–Cherbourg link. In September 2011 she was withdrawn again from operations and in April 2012 she was chartered to DFDS Seaways to operate between Dover and Calais as the *Deal Seaways*. In November 2012 she returned to Brittany Ferries and was renamed *Barfleur* once again. She resumed the Poole–Cherbourg service in March 2013 replacing the *Cotentin* but offering a service for both freight and passengers.

Kvaerner Masa-Yards, Helsinki, Finland, 1992
20,133g / 157.6 x 23.3 m / Twin screw / 19.5 knots
1,212 pass. / 550 cars / 1,530 lane metres

Condor Vitesse - 2001

Incat Tasmania, Hobart, Australia, 1997
5,007g / 86.6 x 26 m / Quadr. waterjet / 40 knots
800 pass. / 200 cars
Brittany Ferries service: 2001-2004

While not chartered or owned by Brittany Ferries, this craft was operated jointly during the summer season by Brittany Ferries and Condor, between Poole and Cherbourg between 2001 and 2004. Built as Incat 044 in Australia the vessel operated on Condor's Channel Islands operations until 2015.

Coutances - 2002

Ateliers et Chantiers du Havre, France, 1978
2,736g / 109.7 x 17.5 m/ Twin screw / 18 knots
58 pass. / 64 trailers / 800 lane metres
Brittany Ferries service: 2002-2008

The Coutances was delivered to Truckline in 1978 for their Cherbourg–Poole service. She was lengthened in 1986, with growing demand for freight on the route. In 2007, after the takeover of the company by Brittany Ferries, she operated on the Caen–Portsmouth service. In May 2008 she made her last commercial sailing with the company; she was later sold with her sister Purbeck to Venezuelan interests.

Mont St Michel - 2002

The *Mont St Michel* was constructed by Van der Giessen-de Noord, Rotterdam for Brittany Ferries for the Portsmouth–Caen link. The vessel's design was modelled on the success of the *Normandie* but with larger car and freight capacity.

Her passenger accommodation has a similar layout to that of *Normandie* but with additional passenger accommodation for 60 passengers. In 2016 an additional central funnel was added to accommodate scrubber units. In 2020 she was joined by the *Honfleur* as her new operating partner. During her career to date she has only operated on the Caen service.

Van der Giessen de Noord, Krimpen aan den Ijssel, Holland, 2002
35,592g / 173.9 x 28.5 m / Twin screw / 21 knots
2,120 pass. / 874 cars / 2,250 lane metres

Ferries

MONT S^T MICHEL
CAEN

Pont-Aven - 2004

The *Pont-Aven* was ordered by Brittany Ferries from the Meyer Werft shipyard on the River Ems, at Papenburg, Germany on 22nd February 2002. Her keel was laid down on 9th April 2003, she was launched 13th September the same year and completed on 7th February 2004, ahead of schedule.

She completed sea trials and was handed over on 27th February, making her maiden voyage on 24th March, from Roscoff to Santander.

In May 2006 the *Pont-Aven* sustained damage en route to Santander from Plymouth: several of the forward windows on deck 6 were smashed by a 9-metre wave, which resulted in a number of cabins and public areas flooding. She was forced to divert to Roscoff where passengers disembarked. On 26th May 2006 she returned to service while refurbishment was carried out on board; the forward windows were later replaced with smaller, round porthole windows.

PONT-AVEN

Bri

She has mainly operated on the Plymouth–Roscoff, Plymouth–Santander and Cork–Roscoff routes, but during the winter periods has also covered the St Malo–Portsmouth link in absence of the *Bretagne*.

Jos L. Meyer Werft, Papenburg, Germany, 2004
40,589g / 182 x 30.9 m / Twin screw / 27 knots
2,400 pass. / 650 cars

Vers la Grande-Bretagne et l'Irlande,
notre route est la plus belle

Caen/Ouistreham-Portsmouth   Cherbourg-Portsmouth   Cherbourg-Poole   St Malo-Portsmouth   Roscoff-Plymouth   Roscoff-Cork

TRAVERSÉES
MARITIMES
2005
HORAIRES ET TARIFS
1ᵉʳ ÉDITION

Brittany Ferries
Laissez-vous transporter

Vacances en **Irlande**
laissez-nous aussi vous héberger

Bed & Breakfast   Guest Houses   Hôtels   Hôtels de caractère   Cottages et maisons de vacances   Circuits

BROCHURE
SÉJOURS
2005
IRLANDE

Normandie Express - 2005 (chartered)

Incat Tasmania Pty. Ltd., Hobart, Australia, 2000
6,581g / 97.2 x 26.6 m / Quadruple waterjet / 37 knots
900 pass. / 260 cars

The Normandie Express *is an Incat Evolution 10 catamaran, built as the* Incat Tasmania. *In November 2000 she was chartered to TranzRail of New Zealand and renamed* The Lynx *and placed on their Wellington–Picton service. In July 2003 she was replaced by the 1997-built Incat 86m craft Incat 046 then in Spring 2005 she was chartered to Brittany Ferries to operate on their Cherbourg–Portsmouth and Caen–Portsmouth services and renamed the Normandie Express. Brittany Ferries purchased her in 2007. During 2013 she operated to Le Havre and in 2015 to Cherbourg as well, but as from 2016 she only operated to Cherbourg with occasional operations to Caen and Le Havre.*

2007

Brit

A GREAT C

Apartments & Chalet C

IN

brittanyferries.com

Pont L'Abbé - 2006

Aalborg Værft A/S, Ålborg, Denmark, 1978
14,399g / 152.9 x 24.2 m / Twin screw / 21 knots
1,370 pass. / 470 cars / 810 lane metres
Brittany Ferries service: 2006-2009

Cotentin - 2007

Aker Finnyards, Helsinki, Finland, 2007
22,308g / 167.8 x 26.8 m / Twin screw / 23 knots
213 pass. / 2,188 lane metres
Brittany Ferries service: 2007-2013

Holidays from *Ireland*

Built as the Dana Anglia for DFDS Seaways in 1978 for the Esbjerg–Harwich route, she was constructed at Aalborg Værft A/S in Denmark and entered service in 1978. She sailed between Esbjerg, Denmark and Harwich between 1978 and 2002 before being renamed Duke of Scandinavia for service between Copenhagen, Denmark and Gdansk, Poland. She returned to the North Sea in 2003 to sail between Newcastle and IJmuiden. As the Dana Anglia she appeared in several BBC programmes including the soap drama 'Triangle'. In 2006 she was chartered by Brittany Ferries to replace the Val de Loire, and renamed Pont L'Abbé. In December 2007 she was sold to Brittany Ferries. After only two years in service with the Breton company she made her final sailing between Plymouth and Roscoff in November 2008. In October 2009, the ship was chartered to Moby Line.

Built in Finland in 2007 for the Cherbourg–Poole route, and to open a new link from Poole to Santander, the Cotentin proved to be successful on both routes. However, her operating costs proved to be uneconomic for the company and she was withdrawn from service in October 2013. She was later chartered to Stena Line for service in the Baltic.

Cotentin *under construction at Aker Yards, Finland.*

Armorique - 2009

In August 2005 Brittany Ferries placed an order with Aker Finnyards (now STX Europe) for an €80 million freight vessel, later to become the *Cotentin*. The order included provisional plans for another vessel, which was commissioned in January 2006 at a cost of €120 million.

This vessel was later named the *Armorique* and was built to carry 1,500 passengers for the Roscoff–Plymouth link. She would be identical to

Cotentin up to Deck 5, but with an extra accommodation block being added above and to the stern to include public and accommodation spaces for passengers.

The first sheet of steel was cut on the 30th July 2007 at the STX yards in Helsinki, Finland. She was floated out on the 13th September 2007, before her final delivery to Brittany Ferries in January 2009. She first arrived in Plymouth for berthing trials on the 26th January 2009, making her maiden voyage outbound to Roscoff from Plymouth on the 10th February 2009.

The *Armorique* is the second Brittany Ferries vessel to bear this name; the first being roughly a quarter the size of the present *Armorique*, and operating between 1976 and 1993.

STX Europe, Helsinki, Finland, 2009
29,468g / 165 x 26.8 m / Twin screw / 23 knots
1,500 pass. / 470 cars / 985 lane metres

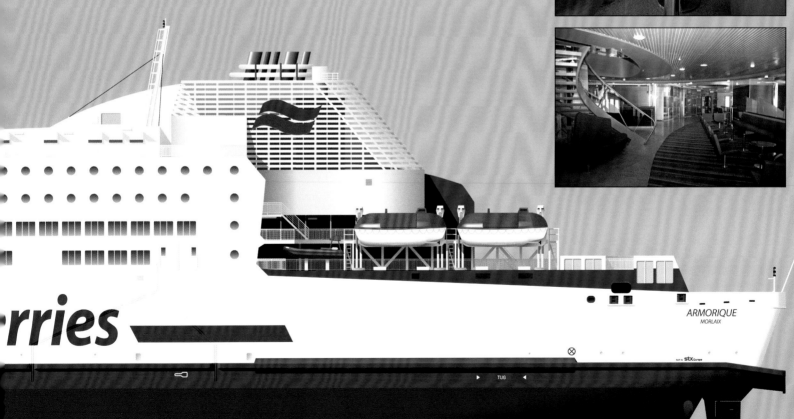

Cap Finistère - 2009

Built as the *Superfast V* by Howaldts-werke Deutsche Werft AG, Kiel, Germany for Attica Enterprises (now Attica Group) for use by Superfast Ferries of Greece, she initially operated between Patras and Ancona and in January 2007 switched to the Patras–Igoumenitsa–Bari route. In 2009 the route became Patras–Igoumenitsa–Ancona.

In 2009 the *Superfast V* was sold to Brittany Ferries, renamed the *Cap Finistère*, and she was placed on the Portsmouth–Santander service,

also operating some sailings between Portsmouth and Cherbourg. In March 2010 she also began operating between Portsmouth and Bilbao and only operated between Portsmouth and Cherbourg during the winter period. She now operates on the Portsmouth–Santander and Portsmouth–Bilbao routes only.

The *Cap Finistère* underwent her scrubber conversion in early 2015.

On the arrival of the second E-Flexer ship for Brittany Ferries in 2022, she may become a dedicated ship for France/Ireland operations or maybe sold.

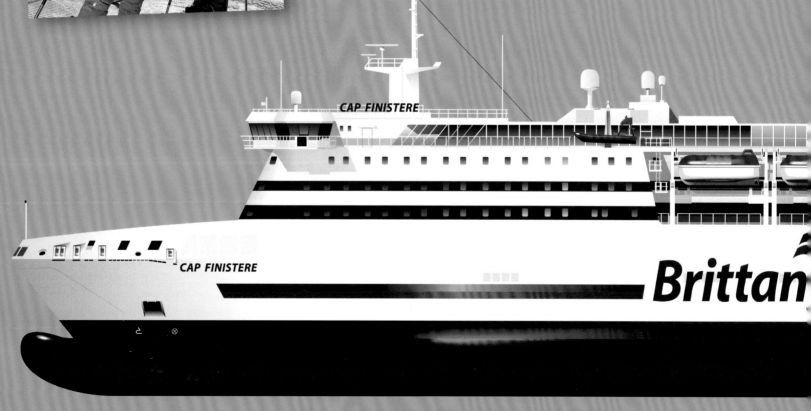

Howaldtswerke Deutsche Werft AG, Kiel,
Germany, 2001
32,728g / 203.9 x 25 m / Twin screw / 28 knots
1,608 pass. / 1,000 cars / 1,926 lane metres

CAP FINISTERE
MORLAIX

Brittany Ferries

Family holidays
in France and Spain

hotels · Disneyland® Paris

2012

Brittany Ferries

France & Spain
Golf breaks

2013

Unbeatable value · unrivalled service · superb courses for *any* golf lover

Brittany Ferries

France & Spain
Cottage & Villa holidays

2013

Choose from *any* of our superb collection
cottages · villas with pool · French gites · Spanish casas · theme parks

Etretat - 2012 (chartered)

Cantieri Navali Visentini Francesco & C, Porto Viro, Italy, 2008
26,904g / 186 x 25.6 m / Twin screw / 24 knots
800 pass. / 195 cars / 2,255 lane metres

Built as the Norman Voyager by CN Visentini, Italy for Epic Shipping of the UK and chartered to LD Lines she operated between Le Havre and Portsmouth and Le Havre and Rosslare. In September 2009 she was sub-chartered to Celtic Link Ferries. Initially she operated between Cherbourg and Portsmouth and Cherbourg and Rosslare, but the Portsmouth service was abandoned in November 2009.

In October 2011 the vessel was returned to LD Lines and placed on the St Nazaire–Gijon route. In November she moved to the Portsmouth–Le Havre service and, following the establishment of the joint LD Lines/DFDS venture, the charter was then transferred to DFDS Seaways. In April 2012 she was sold to Stena RoRo; she continued to be chartered to DFDS.

In March 2014, Brittany Ferries chartered her and placed her on the new 'économie' services between Portsmouth and Le Havre and Portsmouth and Santander. She was renamed the Etretat for her new role; the charter of the ship is due to end on the entry into service of the new 'E Flexer' vessels.

Baie de Seine - 2015 (chartered)

Stocznia Szczecinska im. A. Warskiego, Stettin, Poland, 2002
10,500g / 199.4 x 25 m / Twin screw / 23 knots
600 pass. / 2,060 lane metres

The Baie de Seine was originally built as the Golfo dei Delfini by Stocznia Szczecinska, Poland for Lloyd Sardegna in Italy for service between Italy and Sardinia. However, due to late delivery the order was cancelled. In 2002 DFDS Seaways purchased her, and, during winter 2002/03, passenger accommodation was enlarged and refitted, increasing her passenger capacity from 308 to 596. In June 2003 she was renamed the Dana Sirena, replacing her unmodified sister vessel, the Dana Gloria, on the Esbjerg–Harwich service. In February 2013 she was renamed the Sirena Seaways. At the end of September 2014 the route closed and she moved to the Paldiski (Estonia)–Kapellskär route for a short period prior to being laid up.

In April 2015 she was chartered to Brittany Ferries for five years for their operations from the UK to Bilbao and Santander and Le Havre. She was renamed the Baie de Seine and entered service in May 2015. In March 2020 she was returned to DFDS and replaced by the Connemara until the arrival of the Galicia.

Connemara - 2018 (chartered)

Cantieri Navali Visentini Francesco & C, Porto Viro, Italy, 2007
26,500g / 186.5 x 25.6 m / Twin screw / 24 knots
1,000 pass. / 170 cars / 2,255 lane metres

Built by CN Visentini, Italy, while under construction she was sold to Stena RoRo of Sweden and named the Stena Ausonia. However, before delivery a charter was arranged with Balearia of Spain, she was delivered as the Borja and operated between Barcelona and Palma (Majorca). In February 2010 the charter ended and in April 2010 she was chartered to Ave Line and renamed the Baltic Amber. In October 2010 she was chartered to DFDS Seaways, and during March 2011 she saw service with LD Lines on operations between Marseilles and Rades (Tunisia), then in April she was moved to the Saint Nazaire (Nantes)–Gijon route. She was renamed the Norman Asturias in June 2011. She also operated between Poole, Santander and Gijon for LD Lines. In September 2014 she was working for Intershipping, Morocco on their operations between Algeciras and Tangiers. She was chartered by Anek Lines of Greece in February 2016, renamed the Asterion and placed on the Patras–Igoumenitsa–Venezia route.

In April 2018 Brittany Ferries took a two year charter, she was renamed the Connemara and inaugurated a new twice weekly Cork–Santander service, with an additional service to Roscoff. The Connemara was replaced by the Kerry in November 2019 on the Spanish services from Ireland for twelve months.

Honfleur - 2020

When she took up service in 2020 the *Honfleur* was the most environmentally friendly ship regularly operating in UK waters. The liquefied natural gas (LNG)-powered vessel, with her four engines, meets a standard known as collective diesel-electric-propulsion: this method of propulsion is used extensively on large cruise vessels as it reduces vibration, noise and optimises fuel consumption.

The *Honfleur* is the first passenger ship in the world to be equipped with

on-board cranes that allow 40-feet LNG containers to be lifted into a fixed position. Containers are transported by truck from an LNG terminal to Ouistreham and then driven on board. They are then hoisted into position alongside a fixed LNG storage tank located at the rear of the superstructure. Upon the next call at port, empty containers are removed and replenished with full units.

The *Honfleur* carries up to 1,680 passengers and 550 cars. The vessel operates in tandem with the *Mont St Michel* on the Caen–Portsmouth service. Her passenger accommodation includes 261 cabins, two cinemas, restaurants, boutique shopping and passenger lounges.

FSG Shipyard, Flensburg, Germany, 2019
42,200g / 187.4 x 31m / Twin screw / 22 knots
1,680 pass. / 550 cars / 2,400 lane metres

The Honfleur *being built at the FSG Shipyard in Flensburg, Germany.*

y Ferries

HONFLEUR
CAEN

TUG

Galicia - 2021 / Salamanca - 2022 / Santoña - 2023 (chartered)

These three ships are being built by Stena Line Ro/Ro for Brittany Ferries and will be constructed in China. The ships will be part of the Stena E-Flexer series, which will feature a unique hull design developed by the Swedish company and Deltamarin, with the bow shaped to reduce resistance and the stern shaped to reduce wave making. A total of eight vessels have been confirmed in the series, three of which Brittany Ferries will charter for their Santander and Bilbao operations.

The *Galicia*, *Salamanca* and *Santoña* represent the next step in a fleet renewal and an investment programme worth around €550 million for Brittany Ferries. The company will be engaging Spanish architects to customise the passenger

GALICIA

Brittan

accommodation to reflect the new ferries' association with Iberia. The *Galicia* will will be powered by two MaK M43C diesel engines, with a total power output of 25,200 kilowatts (33,800 hp), driving two propellers that give the ships a top speed of 22 knots. The latter ships the *Salamanca* and *Santoña* will be powered by Liquefied Natural Gas (LNG) offering significant environmental advantages over traditional marine fuels.

AVIC Weihai Shipyard, Weihai, China, 2021-22-23
42,400g / 214.5 x 27.8 m / Twin screw / 22 knots
1,000 pass. / 300 cars / 3,100 lane metres

Chartered ships (names unchanged)

Poseidon - 1973

Ulstein M/V A/S, Ulsteinvik, Norway, 1964
1,358g / 66.5 x 11.9 m / 805 pass.
Brittany Ferries service: 1973

The Poseidon ran the company's first passenger operation on 19th May 1973 between Plymouth and Roscoff. In her first season the ship averaged 120 passengers a day.

Valérie - 1974

1972 / 3,390g
Brittany Ferries service: 1974

Olau West - 1976

Schiffbau-Gesellschaft Unterweser A.G., Bremerhaven, Germany, 1964
3,061g /97.3 x 17.7 m / 1,500 pass. / 180 cars
Brittany Ferries service: 1976

Chartered to replace the Bonanza following the Armorique running aground. She too struck rocks in the channel to St Malo. After repairs she returned to the route until October 1976.

Bonanza - 1976

Ulstein Mekaniske Verksted, Ulsteinvik, Norway, 1972
2,718g / 94.7 x 16.3 m / 750 pass. / 200 cars
Brittany Ferries service: 1976

Chartered to support the Roscoff–Plymouth service in 1976, following the grounding of the Armorique the Bonanza was transferred to St Malo link for a short period in her absence.

Regina - 1979

Dubigeon-Normandie S.A., Nantes, France, 1972
8,020g / 126.9 x 19.6 m / 1,000 pass. / 170 cars
Brittany Ferries service: 1979

The Regina was chartered to maintain the St Malo–Portsmouth link in the absence of the Prince of Brittany from the route with technical problems in 1979.

Normandia - 1979

Kristiansands M/V A/S, Kristiansand, Norway, 1971
2,312g / 118.4 x 16 m / 12 pass. / 636 lane m.
Brittany Ferries service: 1979

RoRo Dania - 1979

Ankerløkken A/S, Frederikstad, Norway, 1972
722g /105.3 x 15.1 m / 12 pass. / 480 lane m.
Brittany Ferries service: 1979

Munster - 1979

Werft Nobiskrug GmbH, Rendsburg, Germany, 1968
4,067g / 110.2 x 18.1 m / 1,000 pass. / 220 cars
Brittany Ferries service: 1979

The Munster was chartered in June 1979 for 20 days following a series of technical problems with three ships in the fleet. She proved to be unsuitable for the St Malo link and was replaced by the Regina.

Faraday - 1980

1980 / 2,932g
Brittany Ferries service: 1980

Ailsa Princess - 1982

Cantieri Navali Breda S.p.A., Venice, Italy, 1972
6,177g / 115.5 x 17.4 m / 1,800 pass. / 190 cars
Brittany Ferries service: 1982

Following the Prince of Brittany suffering a serious fire on board, the Ailsa Princess was chartered to cover the St Malo link until more suitable tonnage could be found.

Viking I - 1982

Jos L. Meyer Werft, Papenburg, Germany, 1970
5,993g / 108.7 x 17.2 m / 1,200 pass. / 260 cars
Brittany Ferries service: 1982

The Viking 1 was chartered to replace the Ailsa Princess on the St Malo route while the Prince of Brittany was off service in 1976.

Stena Searider - 1985

Van der Giessen de Noord, Krimpen aan den Ijssel, Holland, 1973
3,209g / 142.2 x 16.4 m / 12 pass. / 1,000 lane m.
Brittany Ferries service: 1985-1986

Miseva - 1987

Kristiansands M/V A/S, Kristiansand, Norway, 1972
6,057g / 118.4 x 16.1 m / 12 pass. / 552 lane m.
Brittany Ferries service: 1987

Celtic Pride - 1987

Dubigeon-Normandie S.A., Nantes, France, 1972
7,801g / 126.8 x 19.5 m / 1,000 pass. / 170 cars
Brittany Ferries service: 1987

Built in France as the Aallotar for Silja Line, she was later sold to Polish interests and renamed the Rogalin in 1978. In 1987 Swansea Cork Ferries chartered the ship for their operations and renamed her the Celtic Pride. Brittany Ferries chartered the vessel at weekends during peak seasons of 1987 and 1988 to maintain their Roscoff–Cork link.

Gabrielle Wehr - 1988

Rickmers Werft, Bremerhaven, Germany, 1978
1,599g / 108.3 x 17.4 m / 12 pass. / 1,148 lane m.
Brittany Ferries service: 1988

Gotland - 1988

Brodogradiliste Jozo Lozovina Mosor, Trogir, Yugoslavia, 1973
6,642g / 123.8 x 20.5 m / 1,670 pass. / 300 cars
Brittany Ferries service: 1988

The Gotland was chartered to increase capacity on the Caen–Portsmouth link in 1988. She operated in tandem with Duc de Normandie and Breizh-Izel.

Beaverdale - 1989

Rickmers Werft, Bremerhaven, Germany, 1977
5,699g / 116.3 x 18.2 m / 12 pass. / 780 lane m.
Brittany Ferries service: 1989

Skarvøy - 1990

1974 / 3,710g
Brittany Ferries service: 1990

MN Pelican - 2016

Santierul Naval, Galati, Romania, 1999
12,050g / 154.5 x 22.7 m / 12 pass. / 1,690 lane m.

Truckline ships

Poole Antelope - 1973 (chartered)

Dubigeon-Normandie S.A., Grand-Quevilly, France, 1973
988g / 75 x 14.7 m / Twin screw / 11.5 knots
206 pass. / 192 lane metres
Truckline Ferries service: 1973-1976

Dauphin de Cherbourg - 1974

Dubigeon-Normandie S.A., Grand-Quevilly, France, 1974
988g / 75 x 14.7 m / Twin screw / 11.5 knots
206 pass. / 192 lane metres
Truckline Ferries service: 1974-1976

Cotentin - 1975

Suffolk - 1977 (chartered)

Cantieri Navali Felzsegi S.p.A. Trieste, Italy, 1966
1,211g / 94.2 x 14.7 m / Twin screw / 14 knots
Truckline Ferries service: 1977-78

Purbeck - 1978

Tourlaville - 1982

A. Vuyk & Zonen's Scheepswerven N.V., Capelle a/d IJssel, Holland, 1969
885g / 75 x 13.7 m / Single screw / 15 knots
12 pass. / 24 trailers
Truckline Ferries service: 1982-1984

Rickmers Werft, Bremerhaven, Germany, 1969
3,575g / 96.8 x 15.8 m / Twin screw / 14 knots
12 pass. / 410 lane metres
Truckline Ferries service: 1974-1978

Built to replace the two original ships of Truckline, the Cotentin and her sister the Dorset could carry 25 lorries. Both ships remained in service until they were replaced by Purbeck and Coutances in 1978.

Société Nouvelle des Ateliers & Chantiers du Havre, France, 1978
2,736g / 109.7 x 17.5 m (1986: 6,507g / 125.5 x 17.5 m)
Twin screw / 18 knots / 58 pass. / 60 trailers
Truckline Ferries service: 1978-1994, 1997, 2000-2003

The turning point of Truckline came in 1978 with the introduction of Purbeck and Coutances: the new ships doubled the carrying capacity on the route. The Purbeck saw charter work for BCIF, Sally Line, Trans Rail and Irish Ferries after her withdrawal from the Poole link. Both she and her sister were sold for further operations in South America.

Ulster Sportsman / Dorset - 1975

Rickmers Werft, Bremerhaven, Germany, 1970
3,575g / 96.8 x 15.8 m / Twin screw / 14 knots
12 pass. / 410 lane metres
Truckline Ferries service: 1974-1978

Normandie Shipper - 1989

A. Vuyk & Zonen's Scheepswerven N.V., Capelle a/d IJssel, Holland, 1973
3,514g / 142.3 x 18.6 m / Twin screw / 18 knots
36 pass. / 1,050 lane metres
Truckline Ferries service: 1989-1999

Built as the Union Wellington in 1973, she later operated as the Speedlink Vanguard for Sealink as a train ferry before she was chartered and later purchased by Brittany Ferries. Renamed the Normandie Shipper she remained in service with the company until 1996.

The Coutances *(top),* Trégastel *(left) and* Barfleur *(postcard) in Truckline colours.*

Brittany Ferries liveries

1973

1974

1976

1984

2004

2018

In new waters...

The Kerisnel left the Brittany Ferries fleet in 1974 and would go on to operate in Corsica, Saudi Arabia and Greece. Laid up in 2001 in Las Palmas de Gran Canaria as the Agios Dionisios S, the ship remained there for a further 13 years in an increasingly derelict state. She is pictured in April 2013, one year before she was towed away for scrapping. The tow was short-lived, however, and the ship sank north of Lanzarote in May 2014.

In 1975 the Danish-owned Falster was chartered to operate the Plymouth-Roscoff route as the Prince de Bretagne. Brittany Ferries would subsequently order the Cornouailles to a modified design from the same Norwegian shipyard. After her charter the ship resumed her original name before embarking on a long career in Southern Europe, of which the final fourteen years were spent with Ventouris Ferries as the Vega in which guise she is seen at Corfu in August 1999.

After her sale in 1993 the Armorique passed to Chinese owners as the Min Nan. Twelve years later she was sold to Indonesian operator PT Dharma Lautan Utama for whom she served as the Tirta Kencana I and, later, the Musthika Kencana II. In July 2011, whilst sailing from Surabaya to Makassar, a severe fire broke out on the ship's vehicle deck. All 191 people aboard were evacuated but the Brittany Ferries pioneer subsequently sank in the Java Sea due north of Nonggunong on 5th July 2011.

The pioneer passenger/car ferry Penn-ar-Bed was sold in 1984 after a decade of operation. She initially went to Norway for service from there to Sweden but within a year was sold again, to the Greek-Cypriot Marlines and the former Penn-ar-Bed is seen here as their Princess M. In 1989 the ship was sold again, passing through various owners as the Lilly R, Princess and, finally, Jabal Ali 1 in which guise she operated between Dubai and Iraq. She was sold for scrapping in 2004.

After a long English Channel career with Brittany Ferries, SNCF, Truckline, Channel Island Ferries and Condor, the former Cornouailles was sold to Montenegro Lines in 2000, becoming their second-named Sveti Stefan. The ship, pictured at the Montenegrin port of Bar in July 2010, helped to fully re-establish operations following the Yugoslav wars of the 1990s but was sold for scrapping in 2013.

Whilst the 1964-built Olau West enjoyed the briefest of Brittany Ferries careers, spending a short time on the Portsmouth-St Malo route in 1976, her operating life would last for almost fifty years. Her final guise, from 2001, was as the Azzurra and she operated a variety of Adriatic routes before passing to Fergun Shipping of Turkey in 2010. The ship was scrapped in 2013 and is pictured at Bari in 2009.

After a 13-year Brittany Ferries career the Reine Mathilde (ex-Prince of Brittany, Prince of Fundy) was renamed Beauport in 1991 at the outset of a charter to British Channel Island Ferries. The ship would retain this name for the rest of her much-travelled life, which included charters to Comanav of Morocco, Stern Lines of Turkey and the Government of Trinidad & Tobago. She is seen here in 2000 when chartered to Sancak Lines for operation between Brindisi (Italy) and Cesme (Turkey).

The freighter Breizh-Izel was sold to Marlines in 1989 and was substantially rebuilt as a passenger ship, becoming the Duchess M. Engaged in service on a variety of Adriatic routes the ship eventually became the company's final vessel, remaining in service until 2008, latterly on the route from Bari in Italy to Durres in Albania. After several years laid up in Elefsis bay, near Piraeus, the ship was finally sold for scrapping in 2014. She is seen here at Bari in July 2007.

The Bénodet served in Brittany Ferries colours for just one year in 1984/85 but remained in English Channel use with related operators Channel Island Ferries and Truckline until 1990 as the Corbière. Thereafter she returned to the Baltic where she regained her original name, Apollo. In 2000 the ship was sold to the Canadian Woodward Group for use on the lifeline operation between Blanc-Sablon and St Barbe across the Strait of Belle Isle. Pictured in 2006, the Apollo is scheduled for replacement in 2019 when she will be 49 years old.

After finishing on the Portsmouth-Ouistreham route in December 2002 the long-serving Quiberon (ex-Nils Dacke) was purchased by Medmar for use on a new service between Sète in southern France and Palma de Majorca. The route was not a success and the ship, eventually renamed Giulia d'Abundo, subsequently operated on the company's overnight services from Naples. In 2006 she was chartered to the Spanish operator Euroferrys for use between Spain and Morocco, later operating for Euroferrys' owners Trasmediterranea. Laid up in Naples following the 2007 season, a rather unsuccessful post-Brittany Ferries career was ended when sold for scrapping in India in 2010.

The Duc de Normandie was acquired by Trans Europa Ferries in 2005 and has been largely engaged in southern European charter work ever since, principally with Trasmediterranea. Initially renamed Wisteria, following the demise of TEF she passed to Russian owners in 2013 as the Vronskiy. The charters continue and she is largely used on the routes from Spain to Morocco and is seen here departing Tangier Med. port on the hour-long crossing to Algeciras.

The Duchesse Anne was disposed of to Croatian state operator Jadrolinija in late 1996 and, more than two decades later, remains in that company's service as the Dubrovnik. On board, she is largely unchanged from the refit given to the ship when she entered Brittany Ferries service in 1988. Latterly deployed on the Bari-Dubrovnik service, she is captured arriving at Bari in September 2015.

The Swedish-owned Gotland was employed as second ship on the burgeoning Portsmouth-Ouistreham route in 1988, alongside the Duc de Normandie. The following year she was sold to Corsica/Sardinia Ferries, becoming their Corsica Victoria. Lengthened in 1990, she remains in seasonal operation and can be seen here approaching the port of Nice in 2016.

The Moby Corse, seen at Nice in July 2016, is the former Pont l'Abbé which operated for Brittany Ferries on the Plymouth-Roscoff route for four years, between 2006 and 2009. The ship was something of a stop-gap at Roscoff and was largely unchanged on-board from her previous incarnation as DFDS's Duke of Scandinavia (and originally Dana Anglia). The ship was extensively refurbished by Moby Lines ahead of her introduction on the company's services to Corsica in 2010. The vessel is still owned by Brittany Ferries.

The purpose-built Cotentin of 2007 was designed for use on the accompanied freight routes from Poole to both Cherbourg and Santander. Since 2013 she has been chartered on a long-term basis to Stena Line, operating as their Stena Baltica between Karlskrona in Sweden and Gdynia in Poland. Still owned by Brittany Ferries, the ship is seen here at the Polish port in May 2018.

The Val de Loire (ex-Nils Holgersson) operated for Brittany Ferries between 1993 and 2006 before passing to DFDS for use on the North Shields to IJmuiden service as the King of Scandinavia. She was reunited in the DFDS fleet with her original sister, the one-time Peter Pan, and the two continue to operate the IJmuiden route as the King Seaways and Princess Seaways. The King Seaways is pictured at North Shields in May 2016.

Fleet Index (**Bold** numbers refer to illustrations)

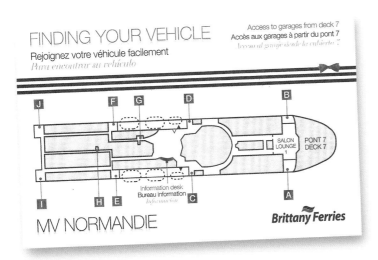

FINDING YOUR VEHICLE

Rejoignez votre véhicule facilement

Para encontrar su vehículo

Access to garages from deck 7
Accès aux garages à partir du pont 7
Acceso al garaje desde la cubierta 7

SALON LOUNGE 1 — PONT 7 DECK 7

Information desk
Bureau information
Información

MV NORMANDIE

Brittany Ferries

Brittany Ferries Holidays

GITE HOLIDAYS IN FRANCE

SELF-CATERING HOLIDAYS WITH YOUR CAR

1997

THE VERY BEST VALUE OF FRANCE

Acknowledgements

The authors would like to express their thanks to Richard Kirkman for writing the introduction to the book and to Matt Murtland for all his help with checking the information on the former ships of the company. Thanks also go to FotoFlite for assistance with a wide range of historical photographs for the book, and to Christopher Jones, Communications Manager UK, Brittany Ferries.

Source of illustrations & photographic credits

Marc-Antoine Bombail: All ship illustrations.

Brittany Ferries: 40 (top), 41, 77 (left), 80), 81, 82, 83.

Andrew Cooke: 38 (bottom), 61.

Matt Davies: 90 (top left).

FotoFlite: 2, 4, 13, 15, 16, 17 (bottom), 18 (top), 19, 20, 22, 23, 42-43, 47, 48, 51, 53, 54 (top left, top right), 55 (top), 57, 68, 74, 77, 79 (top left), 84 (bottom left), 85 (middle, top right).

Darren Holdaway: 40 (bottom)

Kevin Mitchell: 37, 66, 73.

Matthew Murtland: 90 (top right), 91 (top, bottom left), 92 (top left, top right), 93 (all), 94 (all).

All other pictures by Miles Cowsill or from the Ferry Publications Library.

Bibliography, reference books & websites

- *Brittany Ferries 1973-2007* by Miles Cowsill – Ferry Publications
- *Brittany Ferries – 40 Memorable Years* by Miles Cowsill – Ferry Publications
- *By Road –Across the Sea* by Miles Cowsill – Ferry Publications
- *In Waters New* by Richard Seville – Ferry Publications
- *Ferry & Cruise Review Magazine* published by Ferry Publications 1989 – 2018
- http://www.faktaomfartyg.se
- http://www.doverferryphotosforums.co.uk

The Normandie *with her new funnel casing following the fitting of scrubber systems.*